Praise for *Confessions of a Happily Married Man*

"It's all too common today for married couples to part ways as soon as trouble hits. But in *Confessions of a Happily Married Man*, we see a solid relationship that's thriving not because struggles are absent, but because God is present within those struggles. Joshua Rogers shares a timely and Christ-centered perspective on the joys and challenges of marriage."

—Jim Daly | Focus on the Family president

"Reading *Confessions of a Happily Married Man* feels like I've settled onto Joshua and Raquel's sofa as a trusted friend, welcome to observe how they do life and marriage. As the book's title and subtitle suggest, Joshua is forthcoming not only about his missteps in their relationship, but also about the things he has gotten right. Full of humor, humility, and practical guidance for pursuing a God-honoring relationship, this is an exciting new resource for men and women, married or single. Every church library should stock a copy."

—Ann-Margret Hovsepian | Best-selling author

"In my years of doing marriage ministry, I don't think I've encountered a love story like the inspiring journey of Joshua and Raquel Rogers! In *Confessions of a Happily Married Man*, Joshua uses their real-life love story—with all its twists and turns—to provide a practical road map for couples in every stage of life. The goal isn't to have a marriage that mimics theirs but to find new tools, insights, and inspiration to immediately apply to their own marriages. On top of the practical help, this book is wildly entertaining! I read most of it in one sitting and had a hard time putting it down. You'll love this book, and your marriage will be stronger because of it!"

—Dave Willis | Best-selling author and
co-host of *The Naked Marriage* podcast

"Too often in our culture, marriage is understood in ideal rather than real terms. We need more books like this that describe marriage as it really is: the imperfect union of two imperfect people, a union God uses for our sanctification and growth. Joshua Rogers's honesty, vulnerability, and superb storytelling skills will encourage readers to see marriage for what it really is—and what it really can and should be."

—Karen Swallow Prior | author of *On Reading Well* and *Fierce Convictions*

"If you've been married for any length of time, you will find yourself in this book. In pulling back the curtain on his own imperfect marriage, Joshua Rogers creates space for us to reflect honestly on our own. Rogers is a master storyteller with a knack for relaying anecdotes in a way that is profound and often hilarious. His insights will leave you with a deeper appreciation of your marriage and clearer vision to see the ways God is at work in it. This happily married man highly recommends it!"

—Drew Dyck | contributing editor to CTPastors.com,
author of *Your Future Self Will Thank You*

"In *Confessions of a Happily Married Man*, Joshua Rogers gives us an honest and eloquent account of the difficult but happy task of making a marriage work. It sizzles with energy, surprises with humor, and over-flows with Christian wisdom. Buy this book!"

—Bruce Ashford | Southeastern Seminary provost and professor,
coauthor of *The Gospel of our King*

"About a decade ago, when I stumbled upon the writings of Joshua Rogers, I was immediately drawn to his refreshing honesty, outspoken truth, and real-world relationship advice. In *Confessions of a Happily Married Man*, Joshua paints an unvarnished yet striking picture of one typical Christian marriage: his own. Inviting the reader to learn from his mistakes and peek in on tender moments between him and his wife, Raquel, Joshua shows us that the relational challenges marriage brings can both be overcome and take the relationship to new heights. Through humor and vulnerability, Joshua reminds us that God is up to more in our marriages than we can see or even imagine, and He will do great things when we submit ourselves to Him."

—Suzanne Hadley Gosselin | author of *Grit and Grace*

"A great read for those who have been married for a while and even better one for newlyweds or engaged couples. In most marriages, husbands perceive they are out on a limb when problems occur, and they begin feeling vulnerable and alone. In Joshua Rogers's book, he crawls out on the limb with you, but more importantly, he brings a friend: Jesus. You can't help seeing yourself and finding brotherhood in this book."

—George H. Barr | U.S. Army Colonel (retired)

"Books on marriage can read like repair manuals; and often they overpromise. Reading Joshua Rogers's book is a refreshing surprise. It's disarmingly honesty, undergirded by a thoughtful spirituality, and offers no false assurances for five easy steps to fixing the mess many marriages find themselves in. Joshua tells his story of learning to be married well in a way that makes me want to listen more deeply to God, to my own story, and to my husband's. Well done and much needed!"

—Sally Breedlove | Author and cofounder of JourneyMates

"So many of us are tempted to think we are alone in our struggles, particularly in marriage. Joshua Rogers writes with tears, laughter, and Christ-centered passion, helping us understand through his and Raquel's story that we are not alone. *Confessions of a Happily Married Man* will help deepen your faith and intimacy in your marriage. After reading this book you will see why Joshua is one of the most widely read online writers today."

—Aaron Graham | The District Church (Washington, DC) lead pastor

"Hearing one another's stories helps us remember that we are not alone. In *Confessions of a Happily Married Man,* Joshua Rogers comes alongside us and shares the story of his marriage, reminding us of the bigger story in the process. Artistically and beautifully written, you will cry and laugh and ultimately look where Joshua is pointing: to Jesus."

—Rachel Wilhelm | singer/songwriter: *Songs of Lament,*
Redeemer Anglican Church (Atlanta) director of worship arts

"Any counselor will tell you that the journey is more important than the destination, but all too often books on marriage focus on where you're trying to end up (a great marriage) rather than the lifelong process of growing as a couple. Joshua Rogers offers a unique, male perspective about marriage, confessing his own misconceptions, mistakes, sins, and the joys of growing as a husband. When you read a book that focuses on the destination, you feel the pressure to arrive. When you read this book, you think, *I could learn and grow like that too.*"

—Brad Hambrick | The Summit Church (Durham, NC) pastor of counseling, *Becoming a Church That Cares Well for the Abused* general editor

"For many of us, married life is often complicated and messy. In *Confessions of a Happily Married Man*, we find out that God is doing so much more in our ordinary, day-to-day married lives than we usually notice. With refreshing honesty and vulnerability, Joshua shares stories from his own marriage and encourages couples to consider how God may be working in their marriages as well. May you find fresh wisdom and insights into ways that God is deep at work in your own marriage."

—Winfield Bevins | Author of *Ever Ancient, Ever New* and *Marks of a Movement*

"Joshua Rogers's transparency is refreshing and authentic. He beautifully balances the messiness of marriage, never sugar-coating it yet maintaining its sweetness. Singles and newlyweds would gain much wisdom from this book."

—Shayla Ortiz | Author of *Praying Through Singleness*

"Joshua Rogers's personal stories and insights about real married life will strengthen your soul and your marriage. This book is refreshing and encouraging!"

—Bill Gaultiere, PhD | Soul Shepherding founder and author of *Your Best Life in Jesus' Easy Yoke*

Confessions of a Happily Married Man

Finding God in the Messiness of Marriage

Joshua L. Rogers

WORTHY®
PUBLISHING
New York • Nashville

Worthy
Hachette Book Group
1290 Avenue of the Americas, New York, NY 10104
worthypublishing.com
twitter.com/worthypub

First Edition: December 2019

Worthy is a division of Hachette Book Group, Inc. The Worthy name and logo are trademarks of Hachette Book Group, Inc.

The publisher is not responsible for websites (or their content) that are not owned by the publisher.

Published in association with the literary agency of Wolgemuth & Associates.

Unless otherwise noted, Scripture quotations are taken from the Holy Bible, New International Version®, NIV®. Copyright ©1973, 1978, 1984, 2011 by Biblica, Inc.™ Used by permission of Zondervan. All rights reserved worldwide. www.zondervan.com. The "NIV" and "New International Version" are trademarks registered in the United States Patent and Trademark Office by Biblica, Inc.™ | Scripture quotations marked ESV are taken from The Holy Bible, English Standard Version® (ESV). Copyright © 2001 by Crossway, a publishing ministry of Good News Publishers. Used by permission. All rights reserved. | Scripture quotations marked KJV are taken from the King James Version of the Bible. Public domain. | Scripture quotations marked NKJV are taken from the New King James Version®. Copyright © 1982 by Thomas Nelson. Used by permission. All rights reserved. | Scripture quotations marked NRSV are taken from the New Revised Standard Version Bible, copyright © 1989 National Council of the Churches of Christ in the United States of America. Used by permission. All rights reserved. | Scripture quotations marked NLT are taken from the Holy Bible, New Living Translation, copyright © 1996, 2004, 2015 by Tyndale House Foundation. Used by permission of Tyndale House Publishers, Inc., Carol Stream, Illinois 60188. All rights reserved. | Scripture quotations marked MSG are taken from THE MESSAGE, copyright © 1993, 2002, 2018 by Eugene H. Peterson. Used by permission of NavPress. All rights reserved. Represented by Tyndale House Publishers, Inc.

Cover design by Kent Jensen, Knail
Print book interior design by Bart Dawson

Cataloging-in-Publication Data is on file with the Library of Congress.

ISBNs: 978-1-5460-1421-8 (hardcover), 978-1-5491-5027-2 (audio download), 978-1-5460-1542-0 (e-book)

Printed in the United States of America
LSC-C
10 9 8 7 6 5 4 3 2 1

Contents

Foreword

IN JUST A FEW PAGES FROM NOW, YOU'LL READ JOSHUA ROGERS'S "baby monitor story." I won't spoil it for you here, but it's one for the ages.

If I'm honest, my marriage to my wonderful wife, Erin, is filled with volumes and volumes of baby monitor–type stories. Some of them (okay, many of them) are primarily the result of my own mistakes and shortcomings. Erin would be the first to "own" her part as well.

And yet, despite it all, and certainly by the grace of God, we're happily married.

Happily married . . . a phrase that Joshua Rogers uses in the title of this book. You and I have heard this expression countless times. That's the dream. That's the goal! When husbands and wives join themselves in this holy covenant before God and man, "happily married" is what they're after. No one wants to be *unhappily* married.

Sure, during the traditional wedding ceremony we make vows to love one another "for better or worse, for richer or poorer, in sickness and in health." But I think we'd prefer to experience only the good parts of those scenarios—better, richer, healthy. Right?

Of course, that's not the reality. Few would argue that marriage is actually a magical utopia of better, richer, healthier. At least not all the time. Why? Because we're sinners! You're a sinner, and so is your spouse. When two sinners get married, there's gonna be friction. Just ask Erin!

Unfortunately, as Christians we often excel at pointing out the sins and shortcomings of others while conveniently ignoring our own glaring deficiencies. This can be especially true in marriage. We tend to obsess about every little speck in our spouse's eye while remaining oblivious to the plank in our own. (See Matthew 7 for Jesus's thoughts on this issue.)

A happy marriage, then, is not a relationship in which both spouses are perfect. If perfection were the goal, we'd be in trouble. A happy marriage is rather a relationship marked by humility, forgiveness, and grace. Over and over again.

At Focus on the Family, where I spend most of my time, Joshua knows that we have developed a series of "12 Traits" that we believe best characterize a thriving marriage, disciplines that all married couples should cultivate. These are not for perfect people. They're for sinners. They're for husbands and wives committed to pushing back against their own selfish tendencies to pursue a marriage marked by that same humility, forgiveness, and grace.

This book is the perfect ramp up to these. Here's a brief summary of each trait:

1. Lifelong Commitment—Marriage was created by God and designed to be an arrangement that lasts a lifetime, "until death do us part."

2. Spiritual Intimacy—A shared spiritual commitment is a strong predictor of marital success.

3. Communication—A strong marriage is built upon a solid foundation of positive communication and open, honest, empathetic interactions.

4. Healthy Conflict—A conflict-free marriage is likely not a healthy marriage. Thriving couples understand that disagreements can actually help strengthen their relationship and deepen their intimacy.

5. Cherishing—Cherishing your spouse is an attitude of the heart, a resolve to see the best in him or her even when the road gets rough.

6. Nourishing—Nourishing is an action; it involves communicating love in a way your spouse finds meaningful.

7. Quality Time—It's tough in our fast-paced world, but thriving couples spend quality time together and prioritize date nights and other opportunities to simply enjoy one another.

8. Physical Intimacy—You've probably heard it said that sex is the glue that helps hold couples together. It's true. It might look different for each marriage, but couples who embrace a healthy attitude about sexual intimacy increase their chance of success.

9. Shared Responsibility—This might look different for

each marriage, too, but thriving couples understand that they are on the same team and that they've been given the privilege of working *together*. Success isn't about what benefits *him* or *her*; it's about what benefits *us*.

10. Coping with Challenges—As if the challenge of two sinners being married to one another wasn't enough, there are also *external* pressures that will impact every marriage. Thriving couples can learn how to not only cope with crisis but to grow from it.

11. Healthy Individuals—A marriage can only be as healthy as the two individuals contributing to it. Thriving husbands and wives commit themselves individually to a lifetime of spiritual, emotional, physical, and mental growth.

12. Community Minded—Married couples aren't meant to live in isolation. They need to surround themselves with community, both for the support it gives them and the support they can offer others.

Why am I outlining these traits here? Because whether he realizes it or not, Joshua Rogers actually demonstrates many of them in the pages of *Confessions of a Happily Married Man*. I appreciate the transparency with which he shares some of the struggles he and Raquel have faced over the years . . . including that baby monitor story! (It's fantastic. You'll see.)

At one point in this book, Joshua admits that he's not a "relationship expert," despite being introduced as one by an Australian TV host. And that's a good thing. Maybe we don't need more relationship experts. Maybe we need regular, real-life people who are living out God's good gift of marriage even in imperfect and sometimes painful ways.

You'll relate to this page-turning book. I guarantee it. Joshua and Raquel have faced some unique struggles. And some common ones. You will recognize your own marriage in some of these pages. This book is a reminder that every marriage gives us the opportunity to grow in Christ. And to *be* Christ to our spouse. And to reflect Christ to a world that desperately needs Him.

That's a high calling and an awesome privilege for married sinners like you and me!

Greg Smalley, Psy.D.
Focus on the Family VP of Marriage & Family Formation,
coauthor of *Crazy Little Thing Called Marriage*

INTRODUCTION

The Story We Absolutely Had to Tell

ON VALENTINE'S DAY LAST YEAR, I HAD A CONVERSATION THAT led to one of the most consequential decisions of my marriage: My wife and I decided to tell our story in this book.

To be clear, I initially had no interest whatsoever in writing a book. My heart was broken over my dad dying. I was still suffering from the psychological aftershocks of doing an extreme treatment for a chronic illness. I also had a demanding job as a civil defense attorney that was pulling me away from being the husband and father my family needed. I felt drained.

But on February 14, dear friends came to visit unexpectedly, and after a family Valentine's dinner of roasted chicken and fries, my friend Josh looked at me and said, "Have you ever thought about taking your articles and making a book out of them?"

I guffawed, but Josh was so enthusiastic about it that by the time the conversation was over, I believed that some of my stories about marriage could bless readers—maybe people needed to hear real stories from a happily married man. Maybe a few of the hard lessons I had learned could help others.

Three days later, a network news website published one of my pieces about maintaining a forgiving heart toward your spouse. I got an email from a reader named Vincent who complimented my writing and added, "I think you should write a book with all of your articles. It will certainly help a lot of couples."

I began thinking, *Wow. Two times in three days. What if God really does want me to take my articles and make a book out of them?*

An hour after Vincent's message, I called one of the editors at the network and asked if he could make a small correction to my article. He made the change, complimented my writing, and said, "Have you ever thought about taking your articles and making a book out of them?"

That was three people in three days who were saying the same thing: *Take your articles and make a book out of them.* I had no doubt at that point: God was up to something.

I emailed a friend and told him that I believed God wanted me to write a book about marriage, but I needed to get an agent. Thirty minutes later, I received an email from a reputable book agent named Robert Wolgemuth. He had read my piece, looked through some of my other articles, and liked what he'd seen. "Would you be open to a conversation about working with an agency like ours to write a book?" his message read. "This would be our honor."

I read the email in a stupor. Then I looked up from my phone at my wife and said, "Raquel, this is crazy. I'm going to write a book about marriage."

When Robert and I talked on the phone a couple of hours later, we marveled at the way the Lord had brought everything together. I described my book idea to him and, although he liked it, he had one concern. "Are you sure your wife will be OK with this?"

Raquel and I prayed about whether to move forward, and after taking it to God, we came to the conclusion that He was calling us to it.

"Are you sure you're willing to put all of this out there?" I asked.

"Yes," she said. "So many married people out there are hurting, and they feel alone. If our stories can help them notice how God is at work, even in the messy stuff, it's worth it."

Raquel and I began brainstorming about the book and came to the big question of how the book would begin. It would have to be with a story. We looked at each other and knew, without a doubt, which one: the baby monitor story.

Baby Monitor Nightmare

Three months after our first daughter was born, Raquel and I went on a trip to visit Raquel's grandmother in Puerto Rico. It was a nice trip overall—unless you count ten infamous minutes that occurred at her grandmother's apartment. What happened in that little span of time is by far the most awful, humiliating moment of our marriage.

We weren't our best selves with each other, and by that I mean we were frequently "acting ugly" as they say in Mississippi, where I grew up. A lot of it had to do with the fact that Raquel's hormones were "out of control" (her words, not mine) and she was exhausted from trying to keep our new baby girl on a rigid sleeping and eating schedule.

We managed to hold things together when we were around her family, but when we were in the car alone, we would bicker about—well, pretty much everything. The worst was when we were driving around the island in the compact Toyota Corolla we had rented. Raquel sat in the passenger seat and kept telling me how fast to drive, which lane to be in, and whether to turn left or right. I would raise my voice and tell her to get off my back, and then I would remember our baby sleeping in the car seat and hope we weren't somehow scarring her subconscious with all our bickering. But it wasn't the driving drama that sent us over the edge—it was a baby dedication, of all things.

We thought it would be nice to honor Raquel's grandmother by dedicating our daughter at church on the following Sunday. Things got messy on Thursday, though, when Raquel's aunt asked us to sing a couple of duets in Spanish at the service. Raquel and I speak Spanish and sing, but we had no idea what songs to sing or where in the world to find accompaniment music. I quietly (and with a touch of irritation) shared these concerns with Raquel one afternoon in her grandmother's apartment, and she swiftly accused me of having a bad attitude. Before long, we were having a whispery argument that kept getting louder, so we decided to go to the guest room to hash it out.

Once we closed the door, our tempers flared. At first, we argued about the baby dedication performance; then we launched into more general accusations of each other's faults. Adjectives like *hypercritical, hypersensitive, lazy, controlling,* and *stubborn* flew back and forth, until suddenly, in the middle of a sentence, Raquel froze and stared at the baby monitor, which was right next to us. We simultaneously had the same thought, but I was the first to speak.

"Oh my goodness," I said. "The baby monitor is right next to you—it's on!" This was significant because the speaker for the baby monitor was sitting in the living room, and Raquel's grandmother and aunt were home.

"Don't worry," I said, breathing a sigh of relief. "I just realized I turned it off right before we came in here."

We continued rehashing our grievances until we got tired of arguing, and Raquel left the room. That's when she walked into the living room and saw that the monitor speaker was, in fact, still on. She looked at it, hoping she was mistaken, but then she heard me rustling about in the room. She looked around and noticed her aunt walking down the hall toward her bedroom and heard her grandmother clinking pots in the kitchen.

Raquel's heart sank as she turned off the monitor and returned to the guest room. "I just went to the living room, Joshua. You didn't turn the baby monitor to the 'off' position. You turned it to *voice activation*."

We started arguing over whose fault it was that the baby monitor had been left on. It didn't matter by that point, though. We had just given her family a peek at what we were really like behind closed doors, and we couldn't take it back. We were exposed, ashamed, and more aware of our weaknesses as a couple than ever.

The Other End of the Baby Monitor

Welcome to the other end of the baby monitor, where you're about to listen in on the life of a happily married man who's learned almost every lesson about marriage the hard way.

I want to assure you that my wife and I have many cringe-worthy episodes in our marriage that would be far more embarrassing if they were broadcast on a baby monitor. We also have moments that would make the eavesdropper laugh and cry and want to apologize to his or her spouse for being unloving. My favorite moments, however, are the ones in which I can step back and say, "You were in *that*, God? Really?"

Your marriage has those moments every day, though you might not recognize them. From the day you and your spouse said hello for the first time to the absurd argument you had last week, He's in it all. And with just a little bit of attentiveness, you'll notice Him at work, using ordinary life as His tool to craft you and your marriage into everything He planned it to be.

My prayer as you read this book is that you'll notice God in the frustration of pointless arguments, the tender moments of spiritual and physical intimacy, the negotiations over who's in charge, the conflicts over the in-laws, and the dark nights of your souls when all you have is each other. More than anything, I want this book to encourage you to sit with Jesus on the other end of your baby monitor, to invite Him to listen in and point out the moments that you don't even realize are significant. Those moments are happening all the time, whispering His name more often than you may have ever noticed.

You're the Expert

One time I appeared on a morning show in Australia via satellite to talk about the value of giving your spouse a performance review (there's more about that later on in the book). I came home and watched the interview with Raquel online and caught something I had missed during the taping: They had introduced me as "relationship expert Joshua Rogers."

When Raquel and I heard that, we burst out laughing. Regardless of what an Australian morning show host may call me, I can assure you that I'm *not* a relationship expert. I'm not even an expert at my own marriage. I'm just an observer, a happily married man who has discovered a great deal about my marriage (and myself) by paying attention to what God is doing in my day-to-day married life. If that makes me a "relationship expert," then I'm an expert, and I'm hoping this book will make you one too.

So, let's go. Let's turn on the baby monitor and see what we discover. If my experience is any indicator, you'll be as pleasantly surprised as I have been to find God in the messiness of marriage.

1

In the Beginning

I WAS TWENTY-FOUR YEARS OLD AND HAD FINALLY MET THE woman who was "the one." Granted, she was a friend of a friend and I barely knew her, but I could just feel it—she was *it*.

The woman sat across from me at the sandwich shop. Ten minutes into the conversation, I popped the question: "So, when do you see yourself getting married?"

She looked down and seemed flushed—perhaps uncomfortable.

"Well, um, I hadn't really been thinking about that. I just got out of a long-term relationship a couple of months ago and— I don't know when I'll get married."

I sensed that I may have overstepped my bounds.

"I wasn't asking because I think we're going to get married or anything—goodness no," I said. "I mean, this is our first date, right? Of course, I wouldn't have asked you out if I didn't think you were marriage material—but um, anyway—marriage is so far off for me. I mean, I probably won't even get married until after I graduate from law school in a year and a half."

The date went downhill from there, and, as would be the case with almost every other woman I went out with before I met my wife, no second date came of it.

I had issues.

Carrying Extra Baggage

To understand the misconceptions I had about marriage as a young man requires us to look back on some of my foundational years.

Some of my most vivid memories of childhood—both positive and negative—are of my parents' relationship. The happiest memories of our family involve music. Mom and Dad, both talented singers, raised us around Southern gospel, worship choruses from the Jesus Movement, and kids' songs from Psalty the Singing Songbook albums. Mom and Dad had a beautiful, harmonic blend and would often sing duets at church. One song in particular stands out in my memory: "I Am Loved," a 1980s Christian ballad in which the singing couple declare their affection for each other and God's love for them. I can still see Mom and Dad on the stage gazing at each other and then turning to the congregation to sing, "We are free to love each other, we are loved."

As much as Mom and Dad may have loved each other and Jesus, they ultimately couldn't survive the storms they weathered during the early years of their marriage. This included Dad's nervous breakdown after the two children from his first marriage died when the small plane they were traveling in crashed into the Gulf of Mexico. Things had already been hard before that, but as Mom later said, "It's like he stopped wanting to live after the kids died."

For thirteen years I watched my dad free-fall through mental and emotional instability that's best summed up by a play on the words from an old nursery rhyme: "When he was good, he was very, very good; and when he was bad, he was horrid."

On the one hand, Dad would make breathtaking declarations of love for our mother and cause us to blush by kissing her in front of us. He rolled on the floor with us and made us laugh with his jokes until we could hardly breathe. We went on hikes with him for what felt like miles and miles, listening to him give us tours of nature's cathedral out in the boondocks of Mississippi. Dad could, best of all, make Scripture come alive for us with the most vivid descriptions from his wild imagination.

The confusing part was how, at the same time, his presence was so emotionally disorienting. Dad moved in and out of the home four different times—not for another woman but in search of peace for his troubled mind. When he was home, he was unemployed for long stretches of time during which he would go from the joyful, fun dad to a brooding, overweight, angry version of himself. We were frequently on the receiving end of tirades in which he called himself the "king" of our home. This occasionally involved absurd demands, such as him ordering Mom to show him respect by purchasing bigger hot dogs when she went grocery shopping.

Mom spoke positively of Dad when I was a boy, even when he moved out. In doing so, she lent her dignity to him—until she didn't. When I hit adolescence, her dedication to preserving his reputation began wearing thin. She couldn't really protect it anymore anyway. She, my brother, and I were living with Dad's brokenness every day; and eventually, she got to the point where she could barely look at him when we were in the same room.

When Dad finally followed through on a threat to leave us for the fifth time, Mom shut the door behind him and never let him in again. Cinderella finally threw her glass slipper at Prince Charming, and my brother and I watched it all unfold like a Disney cartoon from hell.

A "Eunuch for Christ"

My parents' relationship warped my view of marriage. By the time I reached college, I refused to date any woman for fear of a "mini divorce." My justification for renouncing all aspirations for marriage was sealed when I heard a guy on a radio show preaching about "kissing dating goodbye." He had a book, which I didn't purchase, and I didn't even hear the whole broadcast. But the ten-minute excerpt I did hear gave me sufficient material to justify my renunciation of dating. Eventually, my new spiritual discipline of opposite-sex avoidance hardened into a way of life and I declared that I would remain unmarried.

"For I wish that all men were even as I myself [unmarried],"
said the apostle Paul. "But each one has his own gift from God,
one in this manner and another in that" (1 Corinthians 7:7 NKJV).

I believed I had the gift of singleness in spades. I was so relationship averse that when I took a spiritual gifts test during my
sophomore year of college, my top "gift," with a perfect score, was
celibacy. I told everyone at church that I was going to be—and I
quote—"a eunuch for Christ." I was kidding about the whole cas-
trating myself part, but otherwise, I was serious. God was calling
me to be a charismatic monk.

The guys at church who wanted to be married were, from my
point of view, spiritual weaklings who didn't have the self-control
to submit their libidos to the Lord. They were of minimal value to
God's kingdom on earth.

Whether I wanted to admit it or not, my dedication to singleness had more to do with fear than faithfulness, and that fear was
rooted in a lesson I had learned from watching my parents' marriage crumble: Whatever benefit might come from marriage was
vastly outweighed by the risk of harm to myself and others.

Better to Marry

The most violent blow to my aversion to marriage came through
a young married couple named Shon and Beth, whom I met at a
church small group.

The first night of that small group, I wasn't sure what to do with
the two of them. I figured Shon probably wasn't saved, because he

had long hair and didn't share any insights during the Bible study. Beth, on the other hand, looked more like a Christian with her modest summer wear and shoulder-length haircut. I wondered why she'd married a likely unsaved man like Shon, but after I had been at the church for a while, I figured out why.

Shon, who was a deeply committed Christian, was just as deeply committed as a husband. He and Beth had everything I could've asked for in a marriage—if I had wanted to be married. They were hospitable, committed to Jesus, involved in church together, and very obviously attracted to each other. And for whatever reason, they invited me into their home and made me feel like I was their favorite little brother in Christ.

One sweltering day, Shon and I had been clearing land for several hours and we finally headed back to his house, where Beth was waiting for us. We were drenched in a grimy mixture of dirt and sweat, and we were both dehydrated.

When we walked through the door, I went straight for the kitchen sink and began guzzling from the tap. Shon didn't get much farther than the door. In the corner of my eye, I saw Beth walk up to him, put her hands on his filthy face, lock her lips on his, and give him a passionate kiss.

To avoid an awkward interruption, I remained at the faucet and waited for the kiss to wrap up.

I waited.

And waited.

And waited.

And waited . . . until they finally pulled away.

When I did turn around, they looked at me like nothing had happened.

Their chemistry was obvious in other ways too. They carried on deep conversations about Jesus with ease, prayed together, and opened their home to hundreds of guests over the years. I was one of those guests even after I graduated from college and moved away to law school. I would stay with Shon and Beth when I came back home to visit my parents; and during that time, I got an even closer view of marriage than I had before. I got to see them work through major decisions, resolve conflicts, raise kids, and still hold on to that affection that I had so admired when I first met them.

All that time, I didn't realize what was slowly happening: I had begun wanting what they had. I had started believing in marriage again.

To be fair, another reason I began to desire marriage was because the gift of celibacy had lost its luster. I wanted sex, and I knew the only legitimate way to get it as a Christian guy was to tie the knot. I had become one of those guys I used to scorn— one of those guys who didn't have enough self-control to keep marriage at bay. My problem was that I didn't have anyone to marry, so I decided to do something about it.

Ineligible Bachelor

After I graduated from law school, I moved to Washington, DC, to practice law. I was ready to tie the knot and had money to spend, so I went on a dating spree. Almost all the women I went out with were from church. My church was on the smaller side, and eventually, I had gone out with half the women at least once. I still couldn't get anywhere with dating though.

On the one hand, I was picky. I couldn't make it past the first or second date without zeroing in on some minor issue that made me question whether the woman was marriage material. For example, there was the woman who went to the bathroom multiple times during our first (and only) date. When I asked a friend of hers about it, I learned that my date reapplied her makeup multiple times a day. That was it. I was done.

On the other hand, I was overeager. Sometimes I would meet a woman and ask her out, and before the date was over, I couldn't contain myself. I would be emotionally gnawing on her ankles, dropping hints about my desire for God to send me the right woman in His perfect time (and by "perfect time," I clearly meant "immediately").

Behind my klutziness at dating, something else was brewing. Joshua Rogers, Mr. Squeaky Clean, started morally compromising. I began having random dates with women who weren't Christians, dabbling with porn, and trying to see just how far I could get physically without having sex.

You'd have never known it if you hung out with me. I was living an above-average churchy life. I attended services every week, helped lead music in the worship band, and hosted a small group at my apartment. But the more I flirted with the idea of sexual promiscuity, the faster I slid into sin—until one day, I couldn't handle my double life anymore. I called Shon and my friend Nick and told them what was going on. I finally faced the fact that I needed Jesus to rescue me from myself.

The heartbreaking thing about my descent into moral recklessness was the feeling that I was damaged goods. I had utterly ruined my track record, and I believed that I wasn't worthy of a good woman anymore. And in my mind, I kept hearing this condemning voice saying, *You might as well give up looking for a wife for a while. It's going to be years before you'll be good enough to be married.* That voice was wrong.

Party Crasher

One day, I was alone in my apartment feeling depressed about my broken state. I had finally confessed my sins to my closest Christian brothers and was detoxing from anything whatsoever that might fan the flames of sexual temptation. As I sat there in the quiet, bearing the weight of my brokenness, a story came to my mind from C. S. Lewis's *The Voyage of the Dawn Treader*, a children's story from the Chronicles of Narnia.

In the bleakest scene from the story, the ship has sailed into the Dark Island, where every worst nightmare comes true. Once the darkness closes in around the ship, everyone realizes there's no way out. As the sailors begin to panic, a little girl named Lucy climbs up to the fighting top of the ship and prays to the great lion Aslan, the Christ figure in the story, saying, "Aslan, Aslan, if ever you loved us at all, send us help now." He answers her prayer with a cross-shaped beam of light that leads the ship out of the darkness.

With *The Voyage of the Dawn Treader* in my mind, I wrote a prayer in my journal. I confessed that I had sailed into my own Dark Island by choice, and I concluded, "Jesus, Jesus, if You ever loved me at all, please send help now." I had no idea how quickly He would answer that prayer.

The night I wrote my prayer, I went to a "hat party" in Washington that was hosted by my friend Shannon from church. Partygoers were required to wear some kind of creative headwear, which in my case was a Panama Jack straw beach hat. I remember dancing and laughing with friends on the dance floor but feeling the heaviness of self-loathing until something, or someone, caught my eye.

An attractive woman walked through the door wearing a red cowboy hat with white fuzzy trim around the brim. I couldn't stop looking at her. (I'm pretty sure I wasn't the only one.)

She walked across the dance floor and to the edge of the room, looking uncomfortable. That's when I made a decision that would change my life. I decided to walk over and talk to the young woman.

"Hey," I yelled over the roar of the music, "my name's Joshua. What's yours?"

"Raquel," she said, smiling.

"Where are you from?"

"My parents are Puerto Rican, but I was born here in DC."

"Do you speak Spanish?"

"*Por supuesto*" ("of course"), she said.

"Me too!" I yelled. "You want to practice on the porch?" (What a pickup line, right?)

She said yes, and a week later we went on our first date.

Failure to Communicate

Raquel and I had a good first date—lots of light banter that sometimes veered off into excessive intensity (we talked about the theology of speaking in tongues, for example). It merited a follow-up date, which was already a significant hurdle for me in light of my lackluster dating history. I couldn't help but notice how comfortable I felt with Raquel, how much more easily I laughed and forgot myself around her than I had with other women I'd dated. I got the sense that she felt the same way. But by the second date, that would be called into question.

We decided to attend a concert at Raquel's church, and while we were waiting for the concert to begin, I pointed over to a couple a few rows away.

"Do you see how she's turned all the way to the left?" I commented. "It's obvious body language. She's not into him."

"Interesting," Raquel said.

I forgot about the couple, but Raquel didn't. Halfway through the concert, she looked over and saw my body distinctly turned away from her to the left (I had no idea). Based on my own words, she assumed I was making a statement that I wasn't interested. She began letting the disappointment sink in. She had thought we had chemistry—apparently not.

To Raquel's surprise, when the concert was over and the two of us got in the car, we actually began having an engaging conversation about our faith. It led her to wonder what was going on in my mind. Was I just being polite? Was my body language during the concert even significant? I, on the other hand, was thinking about fried chicken.

I had gotten really hungry during the concert and got a hankering for chicken tenders. I didn't want to go to another sit-down restaurant, though. I had already taken her out to eat earlier that night, and I wasn't going to pay for us to eat out twice when it was just our second date. I didn't even know if our relationship was going anywhere. Plus, all I wanted was a little snack to tide me over, so I interrupted our conversation and made a nonchalant suggestion.

"Want to go to McDonald's?"

"McDonald's?"

"Yeah, I just want to get a little something to eat, but I'm not super hungry."

This only confirmed for Raquel that I wasn't interested—I mean, what kind of guy would take a woman to McDonald's if he was actually into her? That guy, it turns out, was me.

As we rode together for our romantic interlude beneath McDonald's golden arches, our conversation gathered more momentum. I found myself sharing too much information, as I was prone to do when I got nervous with women. She found herself reciprocating, revealing details of her walk with the Lord that she would normally just share with women in her church small group.

The whole thing was pleasantly unsettling to Raquel. Sure, she was overwhelmed by the heaviness of the conversation, but she secretly wondered if it might be an answer to prayer. She had written a long list of the things she wanted in her future husband; on the list, she had written, "I want a guy who likes to talk a lot and have deep, rich conversations." Be careful what you pray for.

When we reached McDonald's, we settled into a plastic booth under the glow of the LED lighting and kept talking. And as the minutes ticked on, I became more convinced she was into me. There was just something about the way she looked at me as I raked my chicken through the lake of barbeque sauce on my tray. The moment of truth came, however, when I finished the tenders. Normally at that point, I would run my thumb through the sauce and lick it off, and I was about to do it. I barely raised my fingers off the table on impulse, but then I lowered them back to the table.

"If you want to lick the barbeque sauce off your thumb, go ahead," Raquel said with a smile. I was shocked. She could do more than hold a great conversation. She could read my mind.

We followed that date with another and another until we totally lost track of the time we were spending together. All the while, Raquel became more beautiful to me physically and as a person. The problem was that I was becoming more and more uncomfortable about some things I was hiding.

The Truth Hurts

When I was single, people frequently said, "You don't really know who the other person is until you get married." In my case, I knew *for sure* that Raquel didn't even know who she was getting involved with in dating me. I had ended a relationship only a couple of weeks before meeting her. And while I hated the idea that she was only getting to know the attractive side of me, I was afraid to show her the rest.

With every phone call and date, I grew more uneasy with where things were going. The first kiss had happened, the chemistry was building, and I had convinced her I was a swell guy who had a strong commitment to sexual purity.

One day, I called my friend Shon in distress.

"Shon, I feel like I'm hiding from her—that she's going to learn about all my hang-ups and feel like I fooled her into being in a relationship with me."

I'll never forget how Shon responded.

"Before Beth and I got married, I told her some of the hard stuff from my past and it bothered her. When she shared that with me, I said, 'Beth, if you're going to love me, you're going to have to choose to love *all* the things about me, including the unlovely things that God used to get me where I am today.'"

After Shon said that, I took a deep breath and thought about what might happen if I pulled back the curtain. I finally concluded that whatever happened had to be better than the stress of feeling like I was hiding who I really was.

At the Risk of Being Honest

One hot June afternoon, six weeks after Raquel and I started dating, we were sitting on a park bench near the Tomb of the Unknown Soldier in Arlington National Cemetery. In the middle of a light conversation, I abruptly interrupted her and asked, "Can we talk about something?"

She said yes and I realized there was no turning back.

I pulled back curtain after curtain, blurting out everything that had been going on shortly before meeting her, and Raquel just listened. This only made me feel more insecure, and I started rambling more and more until I finally ran out of words to say. I ended my diatribe by saying, "Look, I know I've got lots of issues, and if you want to step away from me and evaluate whether it's a good idea for us to be together, I totally get it and I won't blame you at all."

Then I took a deep breath and stared straight ahead.

"Do you have any follow-up questions?" I asked.

Raquel paused and I knew it was over.

"Joshua," she said, and then she paused again. I turned and looked at her, bracing myself for the inevitable. "I'm not going anywhere," she said. "Thank you for your honesty. I know it took a lot of courage to share all of that, and I think you're a godly man for owning up to all of it and letting me know what you've been feeling. I'd really just like to pray for you right now."

Raquel placed her hand on my back, and I leaned forward on the bench. The tension broke inside, I exhaled, and tears began running down my cheeks. I had never been so honest with a woman, and Raquel's unexpected graciousness and support left me feeling undone. I couldn't process such unconditional grace.

"I know it was hard for you to share all of that, Joshua, but frankly, it didn't shake me up at all. I know it was a big deal to you, but we all have our issues."

Later that evening, we were sitting on the couch at my apartment talking when she said, "Can I talk to you about some things from my past?"

"Sure."

And with that, Raquel began to share her own story of brokenness. She kept looking down as she quietly shared details from her past, and when she finished her story, she looked at me, waiting for me to respond.

I looked her in the eyes and said, "Don't worry, Raquel. There's nothing to judge. If the blood of Jesus doesn't cover *all* of our sins, then why did He die on the cross?"

Raquel breathed a sigh of relief. "That means the world to me that you see it that way," she said. "A previous boyfriend held my past against me. What you just said—I know that's how Jesus sees me."

After a couple more hours of conversation, Raquel got up to leave, and as I was walking her out of my apartment, I stopped her in the kitchen and turned to her.

A thought crossed my mind: *We loved each other today.*

I wasn't thinking about love as a feeling; I was thinking about it as an action. That day, we had literally shown love for each other in the most tender moments of vulnerability. As I looked at her, I figured six weeks was too early to tell her I loved her, but I ignored that perfectly rational thought and just said it, right there in the kitchen.

"I love you."

Tears filled her eyes.

"I love you too," she said.

The tears began running down her face and she buried her head in my chest.

"I have this vision," she said, looking up. "I see the blood of Jesus covering us right now—and all the sins from our past."

Just as Aslan broke through the darkness with a cross-shaped ray of light, Jesus had broken through my worst nightmares and rescued me from what felt like certain destruction. The voyage had begun again, and I had found a new shipmate.

Hidden Skeletons

There's so much baggage that we all carry long before we meet our spouses, regardless of how emotionally healthy our upbringing might or might not have been. We're all broken people who have been damaged by sin—our sins and the sins of others.

Some people are fortunate enough to discover long before they meet their spouses how much their brokenness impacts them. They begin the process of healing, which usually requires us to lean on others for perspective and *always* requires us to return to the cross and remind ourselves that we've been freed from the power of sin (Romans 6:22). Many others never allow themselves to face their brokenness, and they certainly don't reveal it to their spouses. They don't even know they're being motivated by their shame a lot of the time. It's like a thumbtack stuck inside their shoe. They have to hobble along to keep it from hurting. Eventually, it feels normal to limp, and they get angry at people who point it out.

It's unfortunate when spouses hide things about themselves (from the past or present) that make them feel ashamed. I'm not just talking about sexual brokenness either. I'm talking about sin in general—like the time I reluctantly admitted to Raquel that I looked down on one particular person because, in all honesty, I felt superior to the person. It was discomfiting to hear myself say that out loud to Raquel, but there was also freedom in it. I pulled back another fig leaf and took a step further into the intimate space of the Garden of Eden. I was a little more naked and a little less ashamed.

The broken places of our lives provide some of the richest soil for growing in a marital relationship. If we can share areas of sin without fear of judgment, it plants seeds of trust. So, when I admitted to Raquel how I felt superior to one person, it became that much easier to admit that I felt insecure about being judged by another person whose approval I really wanted.

Hopefully, in your lifetime, you'll be able to entrust the real you—all of you—to your spouse. I also hope you'll be the kind of person who will handle your spouse's brokenness with care. Mutually coming to that place will require a lot of courage, but the payoff is priceless: You'll experience the fathomless blessing of being loved for who you really are.

Forging Ahead

Six weeks after telling Raquel I loved her, I decided I wanted to marry her. I knew it was an awfully short amount of time for us to be together before deciding I wanted to spend the rest of my life with her, but I couldn't resist. When I factored in our spiritual compatibility and my growing, unquenchable desire for her, the only thing that made sense was to propose to her. And to my surprise, my closest guy friends, a mentor, and my pastor supported me.

Although Raquel knew I had marriage on my mind, I never mentioned it—at least not explicitly. I referred to it as the "possibility of a permanent commitment." I couldn't bring myself to use the *M* word unless we actually knew we were getting married. She rolled her eyes at me and smiled when I did that.

Raquel and I both knew where our relationship was headed. What we did not realize, however, was that there was a lot more to us than we could see, things lurking below the surface that we didn't even know about ourselves. But we weren't even going to begin to figure that out until we were already engaged and wedding planning caused friction that we never anticipated.

Finding God in the Messiness

In the years before my marriage, I was perpetually envious of people who came from stable nuclear families. It seemed like they got a head start in the thing that mattered the most: the ability to give and receive love without being afraid. I idealized their lives, imagining how much more easily I would've fit in as a teenager if I'd come from one of those families. I would've been more confident. I would've dated in high school, met my wife in college, and gotten married the day after graduation. I wouldn't have been this neurotic Christian guy who pushed women away or desperately tried to generate a connection with them. The only real constant in my life was my relationship with Jesus, and all I wanted was for Him to fix me.

Then I met Raquel.

Raquel actually came from a nuclear family, and yet she, too, was broken. Her family moved around multiple times, and in each new school, she reinvented herself in order to fit in. At one school she would be the smart girl in the advanced classes—at another she would be the preppy girl or the outsider or the quiet girl. She was terrified by the thought of not being liked—not fitting in. By the time she reached her twenties, she didn't know who she was. The only constant in her life was Jesus, and all she really wanted was for Him to show her who in the world she really was.

Little did we know that God was using our brokenness to put us on a collision course to come together. Neither of us had had much success in getting relationships to work prior to meeting each other, but both of us had longed to meet that person who could see through our peculiarities and offer unconditional love. That longing was perfectly timed by God to bring us side by side just when we needed each other the most.

No matter what journeys you and your spouse happened to take on the way to meeting each other, remember that divine intervention was at work. I'm reminded of the scene from another Narnia book, *The Horse and His Boy*. In it, a boy named Shasta and a girl named Aravis are both running away from their homes on horseback when two lions thwart their plans and chase the children toward each other until their horses are riding neck and neck. The children eventually stop their horses, dismount, and, very reluctantly, choose to travel together.

Thousands of miles later, Shasta is alone, lost in a forest, when he encounters Aslan for the first time. As they talk, the boy calls himself unfortunate and then makes an unexpected discovery.

"I do not call you unfortunate," said [Aslan].

"Don't you think it was bad luck to meet so many lions?" said Shasta. . . .

"There was only one: but he was swift of foot."

"How do you know?"

"I was the lion." And as Shasta gaped with open mouth and said nothing, [Aslan] continued. "I was the lion who forced you to join with Aravis."

Just as Aslan chased Aravis and Shasta together (the two eventually married, by the way), Jesus chased you and your spouse together, sometimes using the most unlikely circumstances. When He sovereignly introduced the two of you, you had a choice: go it alone or take the journey together. You chose the latter, and God began writing the epic love story of a romance between two people who never imagined the places they would go. He knew that your journey would require a lot of work, and if you're anything like Raquel and me, you never anticipated just how hard that work would be. As our relationship progressed, we weren't just going to get to know each other; we were going to get to know ourselves.

2

Reality Sets In

It was Raquel's birthday and I had lied and told her that we were going to a performance at the Kennedy Center in DC. To be fair, it really was a "performance" of sorts, but there was only one performer (me) and one prop (an engagement ring).

Asking Raquel to marry me after only knowing her for four months was gutsy, I suppose. But I didn't care. I was convinced that nobody could ever love me like her. Plus, I had biblical grounds for a quick marriage. Like 1 Corinthians 7:9 says, if unmarried people "cannot control themselves, they should marry, for it is better to marry than to burn with passion." We were burning for sure.

While we were committed to waiting for marriage to have

sex, our intense attraction was wearing down our resolve to keep our hands off each other. We did everything we could to tear ourselves apart, including promising ourselves that we wouldn't even sit on the couch together, but we just ended up making out on the floor instead. The physical and emotional chemistry was intense and, at times, too much to bear.

Marriage was, from my point of view, the only solution. If we were going to do things right, we had to tie the knot and we had to tie it quickly. So, there I was, sitting next to Raquel on the River Terrace of the Kennedy Center, getting ready to ask her to spend the rest of her life with me.

We looked out at the Potomac on a cool fall evening on the twenty-first of September with the lights of Georgetown glowing in the distance and the airplanes from Reagan National flying overhead, one after the other.

"It's beautiful," said Raquel.

"Sure is," I replied, hoping she couldn't see my heart pounding through my shirt. "You know," I finally said, "it's your birthday, and I just want you to know that you're the one who's the gift to me today."

"Aw, thanks, Joshua."

I took a deep breath.

"I never thought I would meet someone like you—someone who loves me no matter what, a woman who will stand by me, even when I'm at my worst. So, to show how much that means to me, I wanted to get you a birthday present that will make that clear."

I got down on one knee, took out the engagement ring, and looked up at her.

"Raquel, will you marry me?"

A smile burst onto her face and she looked at me with tears in her eyes.

"Yes!" she said, "yes, yes, yes!"

"Really?"

"Yes!"

I kissed her and then something surprising happened: We both started laughing really hard. We couldn't stop. Just when we thought we were finished laughing, we would start up again. We were drowning in euphoria—at least until the next day.

Wedding Cakes and
Subway Sandwiches

Just twelve hours after Raquel and I got engaged, we discovered something that had been missing in our relationship up until that point: We'd never really had to negotiate much. We weren't prepared for it.

It all started when Raquel and I went to a café in the Capitol Hill neighborhood the next morning. Before we even got our food, I suggested that we have the wedding in three months. This did not go well.

I told Raquel that I was trying to save money by getting married in December.

"The church will already have poinsettias and Christmas lights around the balcony, and we won't have to pay for decorations."

She knew that the real reason I was pressing so hard for an early wedding had everything to do with sex. Although she certainly appreciated that, she couldn't imagine pulling everything together in such a short time. When I wouldn't stop pushing for a December wedding, Raquel finally broke down crying, and I finally agreed to a date in March.

I was startled. I never thought we'd have an argument like that, and I hoped we would never have another one. That was wishful thinking.

The wedding date ended up being the least of our concerns. Our fiscal conservatism—a strength we shared—ended up being a continual source of tension. We wanted to start our lives together with as much money in savings as we could so that we could buy a house, and we were both determined to spend as little as possible on the wedding. We set an inordinately low budget for everything, from the wedding dress to the reception, and determined to make it work. We had no idea how hard it would be.

It was like all the businesses we contacted to help us had a special price for anything wedding related, and it was a high one. Venues, bouquets, monogrammed napkins, caterers, decorations, birdseed, and bubbles could all add up so fast. And the wedding cake—I never *dreamed* how much a wedding cake could cost, which is why I was so grateful when Raquel's friend, a baker, offered to make it for us. It didn't matter, though. If you brought your own cake, most of the venues charged a significant cake-cutting fee.

One day when we were shopping online for a caterer, I had an idea—and I was serious about it.

"Raquel, we could save money on the reception by stringing up Christmas lights in someone's backyard and ordering lots of Subway sandwich trays. It will save all the money on a venue, and Subway won't charge a cake-cutting fee."

When I made the suggestion to Raquel, she just stared at me before saying, "Are you crazy? We're not eating Subway sandwiches and cake in a backyard."

I didn't get it. We still loved each other and had great chemistry—as long as we weren't making any decisions about the wedding together. One minute we would be enjoying a romantic conversation at a nice restaurant; the next minute we would stumble into a conversation about a contested wedding detail. It was all over then.

I would try to persuade Raquel that I was right and refuse to give up. She would respond by accusing me of not caring about how she felt. And in the midst of this, I felt this low-grade grief as I wondered what had happened to the two of us.

Divine Intervention

Mark, my pastor, had no idea what he was getting himself into when he agreed to officiate our wedding and do our premarital counseling. Our wedding was his first one, and I guess he decided he was going to do everything he could to get this one right. He met with us nine times—*nine times*—for ninety-minute counseling sessions. We needed every one of them, and we still remember some of the wise insight he gave us into what it takes to have a healthy marriage.

In one particularly contentious session, Mark said, "Before you say critical things about each other, ask yourself, 'Am I really saying this because I'm seeking to build up the other person and encourage my partner to grow in a relationship with God?' If that's not your intention, you probably shouldn't say it."

"Mark," I said, "it's hard to be encouraging when I feel so discouraged. It seems like the more wedding planning we do, the more controlling she seems to get. I mean, the only thing she let me put on our gift registry was a salt shaker!"

Raquel began crying.

"I may be controlling sometimes," she replied, "but I'm really struggling with everything we have to do, and Joshua always wants to have his say on some of the smallest details. Sometimes he just pushes and pushes and pushes; if I don't push back, I'm afraid he's going to run over me."

Mark looked at both of us like a dad trying to break up a fight between grown siblings.

"It's interesting," he began, "to see how your unique weaknesses are creating this crucible that the Lord is using to expose the places where both of you need to change. On the one hand, Joshua, you can be a bulldozer, which makes Raquel feel cornered. On the other hand, Raquel, you've got far more power with your words than you realize, and you're injuring Joshua through criticism. It's going to take some time and friction to smooth out these rough edges, but be encouraged because the Lord is at work in all of it."

Those words got down deep in us and would resonate for years after our wedding. Our conflicts were normal—maybe even helpful in some ways. God was transforming us, and He was using the friction in our relationship to smooth our rough edges and begin the process of making our relationship one of His works of art. Note that I said He was *beginning* to do that work. He still had a long, long way to go with us.

This Isn't My Life

Raquel and I look back over the squabbles we had over things like Subway sandwiches and backyard wedding receptions and laugh when we share those stories with others. But while they may be funny now, there's an aspect to them that isn't funny at all. We weren't just fighting over wedding details. We were desperately and sinfully fighting for control. We still do sometimes.

It's in the day-to-day negotiations of marriage that we discover whether we're willing to loosen our grasp on the power and control that we so tightly hold on to. That's where we figure out whether we love each other enough to be "completely humble and gentle; be patient, bearing with one another in love" (Ephesians 4:2).

Sure, it's easy to imagine myself standing by Raquel's side if she were to have a terminal illness. But the thought of letting her dictate what chores I'm going to do makes my whole body tense up. Boiling up from my heart come thoughts like, *This is my life. You're not going to tell me what to do.* I'd never admit those thoughts to her though—I don't even admit them to myself—but they're down in there; if there's any question about that, all you have to do is ask me to vacuum the entire house when it's obvious that I'm in the middle of something.

As the years have gone by, Raquel and I are having more and more moments of grace, and that starts with the little things too: paying attention to the tones we use, anticipating each other's needs, and deferring to each other without grumbling. We're seeing that marriage is an endless wealth of opportunities, big and small, to make unconditional love a way of life. And one good decision at a time, our lives are telling the story of a romance that's far bigger than us. It's the greatest love story of all time, and we started telling it on our wedding day.

The Center of Attention

When it came to the wedding, Raquel and I didn't pray about appetizers, bridal dresses, bouquets, corsages, or the dance mix at the reception. It was all about Jesus.

Again and again, we prayed, "Lord, be the center of attention at our wedding. We don't care about anything else. We just want people to have an encounter with You." We also prayed that when people saw Raquel walking down the aisle in her bridal dress, they would catch a glimpse of the bride of Christ, and when they saw me, they would be reminded of Jesus, the church's groom. We had no idea the magnitude of what we were asking. We thought we were praying about a wedding ceremony. Our heavenly Father was listening to us and saying, "You want to represent Jesus and

His bride, do you? That's exactly what I want, too, and as the years go by, you're going to look more and more like them."

One of the most memorable moments of our wedding happened when we both had an opportunity to share our testimonies of gratitude that God had brought us together. I concluded my testimony by saying, "With Raquel, God showed me how much He cares for me, and if I ever wonder again whether God loves me based on my performance, all I have to do is look at her." Raquel ended her testimony with these unforgettable words: "I trust you, Joshua. . . . You have my heart."

All the friction and resentment of the previous five months evaporated and were replaced by a sense of forgiveness and relief. I had been hoping that the ceremony would bring a fresh start to our relationship, and after we took our vows, I felt certain things had finally changed.

This is a holy moment, I thought as we drove to the reception. *God has done a supernatural work at the altar and made us one. Our relationship will never be the same.*

That part was certainly true, but then I had a follow-up thought: *I know we'll have little moments of frustration with each other in the future, but I really don't believe we'll ever have a big fight with each other again.*

God must have laughed out loud.

Finding God in the Messiness

The early tendency of Raquel and me to have conflicts over trivial things was ironic. Our relationship had gotten off to such a good start because we felt that God had shown His great love for us in spite of our poor performances, and we had extended unconditional forgiveness to each other. Now we were failing to give that same love to each other as we zeroed in on each other's flaws. We had to decide whether we really believed that "love covers over a multitude of sins" (1 Peter 4:8).

I wonder when it was that you began to face the fact that you had married another broken sinner. Maybe it was after a pointless argument or the discovery of a critical difference of opinion. Perhaps the offense came through what *wasn't* said: the compliment withheld, the failure to defend, the passive-aggressiveness. In all likelihood you're still dealing with some of those weaknesses you discovered early on. And, if past is prologue, those weaknesses may not ever go away.

The nagging question in all of this is whether we're going to love—really love. Will we extend the grace we need, or will we instead demand the very performance we can't give? If we're going to go down the pathway of love, we've got to be willing to examine our own flaws first instead of assuming our spouses should be the first to change.

It's only when we look inside, examining ourselves before God and honestly confessing our shortcomings, that we can receive His unconditional love for us. In that authentic, humble posture, we'll be able to give the grace we so desperately need. Maybe. The problem is that we're limited in our ability to confess our shortcomings because we often don't even know what they are. That's where we need other people to step in—especially our spouses. If we'll listen to them, they can offer us more than enough material to take before God and pray, "God, have mercy on me, a sinner" (Luke 18:13). And let me tell you, in my second year of marriage, I went on a journey of self-reflection that made me cry for mercy in a way I never had before.

3

Stunned by My Reflection

IT ONLY TOOK SIX DAYS INTO OUR HONEYMOON BEFORE WE HAD
our first post-wedding argument. The heated exchange erupted
over what I was going to wear to dinner.

The resort where we stayed in Mexico's Riviera Maya had
a special five-course candlelight dinner by the sea, and I had
brought my gray suit jacket and pants for the occasion. I thought
Raquel would be impressed with my sleek look.

Raquel stepped out of the bathroom in an elegant, but
casual, black dress. She probably would've brought more layers
if we had realized that evenings at the beach are inordinately
chilly at that time of year.

Before we left the room, she asked, "Are you going to wear that?"

"What do you mean?"

"The jacket. I don't know, it's just . . ."

"What?"

"Embarrassing."

I felt humiliated by her blunt criticism. My sleek look had suddenly become a silly one.

"Fine," I said, and in a remarkably childish move, I pulled off my jacket and tossed it onto the bed.

"That was so unnecessary," she said.

"You must be talking about your comment," I replied.

I wasn't just embarrassed by her response to my outfit. I was irritated. Paradise was lost. I had convinced myself that she wouldn't nitpick at me again after we got married, but as it turned out, she couldn't even make it a week before offering a sour critique.

After we arrived at our table on the shore, we remained silent, and even after the sun went down, we coldly looked away from each other as we ate our appetizers.

That's when things went from bad to worse. The balmy breeze suddenly became cool and the salty, humid air, which had been so refreshing in the sun, began to whirl around us and chill our steak and seafood platters. Raquel and I started shivering, and I put my hands over the candleholder in an effort to warm up (a true gentleman would have offered the candleholder to his date).

Finally, I looked over at Raquel and broke the silence. "I would give you my jacket, Raquel, but I don't have it," I said.

My sarcasm launched us into a series of complaints and denials until finally it got so cold that we weren't able to focus on our fight anymore. We just wanted to warm up, and the whole thing started to seem so stupid—our first marital fight was over my evening attire. I looked at Raquel with a playful smirk and tried to suppress a smile. She looked back, raised her eyebrows, and tilted her head. Then I made history: I offered the first apology of our marriage.

"I'm sorry," I said. "That was really unnecessary for me to flip out like that."

"I agree," she said.

"Do you forgive me?"

"Yes," she said. "It really is cold. Let's get out of here."

And with that, we returned to the room, where we kissed and made up.

Taking Each Other to Court

Raquel can attest to the fact that one of the challenges of being married to me is that I'm a lawyer. And, like any attorney, I don't like to lose my cases. While that attitude has served me well in the courtroom, it has created struggles in my marriage.

In the early days of our marriage, I almost always approached my disagreements with Raquel like they were legal battles. That meant that I used the same tactics that helped me win cases as a defense attorney. This is how it usually worked:

1. Raquel would make a complaint: She would accuse me of doing something that offended or hurt her. For example, she often complained that I failed to clean the shower like I was supposed to. (Shower cleaning is my job because Raquel hates doing it; but believe me, she does her fair share.)

2. I would deny the allegation and offer evidence to support my case. In the case of the shower cleaning, I would remind her that I had cleaned it "recently," and by "recently," I meant that I had done it at some point in the past three months.

3. If that failed, I would consider whether to settle the case strategically. Typically, I would concede a little something to make her back down. For example: "OK, I'll try to start cleaning the shower more consistently." But my commitment to "trying" was intentionally vague. I still cleaned it when I felt like it, which wasn't very often.

4. If my settlement attempt didn't work, I took the case to trial: We would have an all-out battle over which of us was more wrong than the other. By the time somebody won, both of us had lost.

To be fair, I lodged plenty of complaints of my own against Raquel, but they only resulted in denials and almost never an apology. I found it so aggravating. Her seeming inability to utter the words *I'm sorry* made her offenses seem worse to me, and it made my ability to apologize seem so generous in my eyes. I was the mature one. My sins were less significant from my point of view. At least I asked for forgiveness and received a begrudging pardon from her. My pride—the desire to make my best case— had shattered my side mirrors, leaving blind spots all around.

What You Think You Know

Though people say you don't really know who someone is until you get married, what they don't say is that you don't know who *you* are until then either.

When I first married Raquel, I was aware of a lot of my negative character traits, but there's a difference between being aware of your negative character traits and realizing what it's like for other people to be on the receiving end of them. Now I was an adult who was married to another grown-up—one who detected my most vexing flaws and seemed determined to point them out until I changed.

My excessive need for affirmation mixed with Raquel's tendency to point out my flaws was a recipe for persistent conflict. She was, in her mind, loving me by helping me grow with her "encouragement." I was resisting her because I felt like she was constantly trying to nag me into being someone I wasn't. I didn't want to hear her complaints, and I even dodged helpful things she pointed out by accusing her of being hypercritical.

I had a very particular and delicate way I wanted Raquel to raise her concerns: I wanted her to provide multiple positive words of encouragement to balance out her negative observations, and

I told her as much. So, I took offense when the negative feedback continued to outpace the affirmations. Looking back on it now, I realize that Raquel wasn't so much picking me apart as she was simply telling the truth. I couldn't see it for myself, but that dramatically changed when I volunteered to go through a process in which I put myself on trial.

Trial by Fire

During my second year of marriage, my friend Aaron started a three-man small group with my friend Pat and me. A conversation we had during one of those early meetings ended up changing my marriage in ways that reverberate to this day.

Aaron had been reading a lot of material surrounding the topic of integrity, including the book *Integrity* by Henry Cloud, in which Cloud suggests that the reader consider interviewing a few people and asking them to provide unvarnished feedback. I was intrigued.

Aaron handed us the list of interview questions. One particular question caught my attention: "What do you observe about my life that you find distasteful?"

"Yikes," I said. "That could be a hard question to ask someone. But if I did, I would find someone who wouldn't try to spare my feelings. You would definitely go too light on me, Pat. I can't imagine you'd even be able to think of something distasteful about my life."

"Oh yes I could," Pat quickly replied.

I was taken aback.

"Oh really? Do tell."

"Are you sure you want me to say it in front of Aaron?" he asked.

"Sure," I said, feeling uneasy.

"Sometimes I feel embarrassed by the way you speak to Raquel."

"Really?"

"Yeah, it's just kind of demeaning."

I swallowed and said, "Well, I appreciate you telling me that."

At first I felt the familiar sting of judgment, but I pushed through it, trusting that Pat wanted the best for me (and Raquel too). I had just learned something new about myself, and it had been a long time since that had happened. I decided that I wanted to know more.

"I'll do the interviews," I said with determination.

"Really?" Aaron said.

"Sure, why not? What have I got to lose?"

The stage was set for the trial of my lifetime. I enlisted Raquel, three friends, and my pastor and asked them to do the integrity interviews with me, never imagining what it would be like to hear these "character witnesses" testify to me about how much I needed to grow.

When I sat down to interview Raquel for my foray into self-awareness, I took out my pen and paper, and I said the innocuous words that would change our relationship for years to come: "Raquel, the most important thing you can do is to be honest with me. You can't help me if you only tell me part of the truth."

Things started out well. Raquel spoke in a warm, loving tone, describing me as loving, affectionate, and a highly encouraging husband. I smiled and felt relieved—she didn't think I was such a bad husband after all. Unfortunately, the feedback didn't stop there. For the rest of our conversation, she shared all of those things I resisted hearing from her—the kind of stuff that reminds a man how badly he still needs to grow.

I was relieved when Raquel finally reached her conclusion: "I want you to know that I love you with all my heart, Joshua. Regardless of the fact that you need to grow in some areas, I never want to be away from you."

I shook off the interview after it was over. I figured that even if there was some truth to what she was saying, she was probably just exaggerating. I wasn't prepared for what I was about to hear in my subsequent interviews with three close friends and my pastor.

As I met with each of these men, 80 percent of their feedback—positive and negative—was the same as I had heard from my interview with Raquel. I was stunned. Raquel wasn't being hypercritical. She was telling the truth.

Over the next couple of weeks, the revelations from the interviews dominated my thoughts, and I went into a period of soul-searching and low-grade grief. I rehearsed the interviewees' comments in my head over and over again, feeling ashamed and realizing that everyone probably felt this way about me—coworkers, fellow church members, and my other friends. It was so unbearable that I found myself wanting to blame my interviewees for being too hard on me, but I couldn't. They'd done exactly what I'd asked of them.

Something that really got to me was that, in the back of my mind, I knew these areas of weakness were there. The reason I knew was because I had heard people point them out to me throughout my life—even as a child. But I had fended off the feedback, either dismissing it as exaggeration or blaming others for being judgmental. Now I couldn't deny what was right in front of me. These were the people who knew me best, folks who loved me enough to be honest with me in hopes that it would make a difference. Like never before, I knew I needed to change, but I didn't know what that would look like. "Faithful are the wounds of a friend," says Proverbs 27:6 (KJV). My friends had, with love, done their jobs well.

The Gift Is for Others Too

I don't know why I felt like I needed to put myself through the grief of a five-person interview process in order to change (and I don't recommend it for everyone, but if you're interested, you can find a guide in Appendix B). Maybe it was because I subconsciously knew that it was the only way change would happen. My raw, undercooked character needed to be microwaved into a more digestible form.

You don't have to put yourself through the heartache of a series of formal interviews to make the necessary adjustments in your relationship with your spouse (and to make general adjustments to your character). Instead, take a couple of steps to get yourself moving in the right direction, starting with asking your spouse a simple question: "Where do I have room to grow?" I realize that it's hard to ask that question to any person, let alone your spouse—the person who knows you best. It's such a vulnerable act of submission to place yourself under the examination of someone who knows you so intimately, a person who can identify your weaknesses more quickly and accurately than anyone else. What if the feedback leaves a wound that never quite heals?

To be clear, I would never advocate that your spouse put you through the pain of verbal abuse. It's one thing for someone who loves you to speak uncomfortable truths, but it's a whole other thing to live with a person who puts you down, humiliates you, and leaves you feeling unlovable. Do not tolerate the latter. Get help from a trustworthy person or counselor who cares enough to help you set up serious boundaries, if necessary.

Your loving but imperfect spouse will provide feedback that may be poorly executed, but hopefully it will be feedback that is gracious enough to help you grow. That may not be the case—you never know until you try—but don't let that be an excuse to stay the way you are. Take the feedback to the Holy Spirit and ask, "Is there truth to this, Lord?" Then prepare yourself as He pulls back the curtain and allows you to get to know yourself a little better. It might hurt to face some unpleasant realities about yourself, but remember that "the Lord disciplines the one he loves, and he chastens everyone he accepts as his son" (Hebrews 12:6).

His correction may come with the sting of self-knowledge, but it's worth the gift that your changes will bring to other people.

Another courageous thing to do is ask your spouse this question: "What are some ways I'm a blessing to you?" It's almost as terrifying as asking how you can grow. What if your spouse has to think for five minutes before scrounging up a compliment or two? What if you come off looking needy and desperate for affirmation? (Many of us *are* needy and desperate for affirmation from our spouses.) Take the risk. Don't let pride and insecurity keep you from humbling yourself and, in a childlike way, essentially asking your spouse, "Can you please remind me why you like me?" The answers to this question can also provide good material for your times of prayer as you turn your attention toward God and thank Him for the ways He has helped you grow.

Ideally, your spouse will give you an opportunity to reciprocate with helpful feedback, but that's not the point of the exercise. I was surprised when, a few weeks after I interviewed Raquel, she asked if she could interview me. I was honest with her about her tone of voice and the way I was weary of being told what to do all the time. She sat in the living room listening, nodding her head, and offering no defense. In the years to come, I would see my feedback making a difference. Just like me, she has slowly made progress—two steps forward, one step back—but she has stayed humble and teachable. We both have (for the most part).

As Raquel and I have continued to give feedback to each other, we've learned that our feedback is most helpful when it comes from a kind heart rather than from an exasperated one. I can deliver truths "in the tongues of men or of angels," but if I "do not have love, I am only a resounding gong or a clanging cymbal" (1 Corinthians 13:1). We still play the occasional "gong" in our home—we'll never stop growing—but as the years have gone by, there are even more symphonies of grace.

I wonder what you felt when I suggested that you ask your spouse to share how you can grow. How about when I asked you to consider blatantly asking for affirmation from your spouse? Did you feel resistant, like I still do? We need to pay attention to that. It's likely an area where there's work that God can do, and it will invariably come back to an issue of pride.

One humbling thing to keep in mind is that a lot of times—maybe even most of the time—we'll go through life and be clueless about the burden we can be to our spouses, even if they tell us. Basically, whether we realize it or not, we'll require their grace in a similar way that we require it of Jesus. Having that perspective gives us an opportunity to be grateful for the part when they said, "I do . . . for better or worse."

Change Is Good

In the years since the first interview process, I've done two more rounds, and with each one, I've felt more encouraged as the feedback has changed. There are positive responses that I didn't hear before, and there are negative responses that I don't hear anymore.

The biggest impact of the first interview with Raquel was my increased willingness to take her feedback seriously. I used to shrug off any negative comments from her (and there were plenty of them). When I realized that she wasn't alone in her perspectives, I began considering that maybe—just *maybe*—there was some kernel of truth to what she was saying, and it often had an impact on my behavior. For example, I became less likely to talk over people and more likely to listen and ask questions. I also became less likely to take control every time I was in a group and a decision had to be made. She has essentially done a favor for others and for me.

I've made many more changes that have had positive effects on Raquel, others, and me. One of the best examples is a small but impactful change in an area that had never been my strong suit: chores. When I was a kid, I was the little brother who pretended to have asthma to get out of mowing the yard. And when it came to cleaning the kitchen, I'd halfway wipe off the table and light a couple of candles, hoping Mom would applaud my effort to put the extra touch with a little flame. By the time I got married, I hadn't made much progress on the housekeeping front. I was OK with arranging the pillows on the couch and picking up stuff off the floor, but otherwise, I felt like I deserved special recognition for efforts—especially doing the dishes.

I hated doing the dishes. I consistently did a sorry job of it when I was growing up, and things didn't get any better when I moved out and got my own apartment. I would eat my food, rake the scraps into the toilet (I didn't have a food disposal), and throw my plate in the dishwasher without scraping off the crusty stuff. When I got married, we had a deal: If you cooked, you didn't have to do the dishes; hence, I was always the one doing the dishes. I resented every one of them.

"You wash dishes with a bad attitude," Raquel would say.

"I don't have a bad attitude. I just don't like the way you order me to do them."

"The only reason I have to order you to do them is because you don't do them unless I tell you to."

She was right, but it was hard for me to see it. I had grown into gladly mowing our fairly large yard, and I didn't mind changing diapers, so I figured doing these things absolved me of doing other chores with a happy heart. They didn't, of course, and thank God that Raquel kept pushing me to grow up and take responsibility around the house. It wasn't that she was trying to be my mom—she just wasn't going to let me get away with being lazy. Over the years, my attitude slowly shifted until one night a couple of years ago I was doing the dishes and realized I actually took a slight sense of pleasure in it. It was a small way I could make life a little easier for Raquel.

It's the little things that I do with a lot of love that have made a difference as I've bent my will to bless my wife. She juggles so many tasks throughout her day that she has often suffered from anxiety, and this makes it harder for her to be her best self. When I do those small things that relieve mere ounces off her heavy burdens, her heart opens up and it's easier for her to reciprocate love.

In blessing her, I am blessed, and all it took was responding in love to her request that I do something as basic as household chores.

Getting Feedback from God

Raquel's feedback has been invaluable, but I don't think it would've had any staying power if it weren't for the fact that I'm listening to God's voice as well.

The thing that has most challenged my stubborn will in marriage from the beginning is hearing the voice of the Holy Spirit bringing the truth of Scripture to life. I've been reading the Bible and going to church all my life, but more than anything else, it's marriage that has made Scripture come alive to me—sometimes in ways I didn't want.

A couple of years ago, Raquel asked me to run to the supermarket to pick up some fruit before we went over to another couple's house for brunch. I was pressed for time, but I wanted to get the yard mowed so I wouldn't have to worry about it later that day. Raquel came out and asked me to stop, but I hollered over the sound of the lawn mower and assured her that I would get it done really quickly. I was, unsurprisingly, incorrect.

When I got inside, it was too late to go to the grocery store, and Raquel was upset with me. She kept harping on me about how inconsiderate I had been, and I finally offered a half-hearted apology and went upstairs to take a shower.

I was aggravated with Raquel, and I started telling God about it. A few sentences in, however, I realized He didn't want to hear it.

I knew that because the Holy Spirit reminded me of this sobering verse from 1 Peter 3:7: "Treat [your wife] as you should so your prayers will not be hindered" (NLT). No wonder it felt like God wasn't listening. I had been inconsiderate of Raquel, and then I came and shrugged off her legitimate complaint.

In many other moments like this, the words of Scripture have jumped off the page and shown me where I need to change my attitude or behavior. They've also shown me how I'm growing. For example, when I overlook something Raquel is doing that irritates me, the Spirit encourages me by reminding me of Proverbs 19:11: "It is to one's glory to overlook an offense." There are so many other verses that come to mind as well, including the following:

Be kind and compassionate to one another, forgiving each other, just as in Christ God forgave you. (Ephesians 4:32)

Let the words of my mouth and the meditation of my heart be acceptable in Your sight, O LORD, my strength and my Redeemer. (Psalm 19:14 NKJV)

The Holy Spirit has used these passages to inspire confessions, apologies, and loving confrontations that would've never happened otherwise. I know it's going to be a lifetime journey for Raquel and me to learn how to bear all things, believe all things, hope all things, and endure all things (1 Corinthians 13:7), but having the Scripture in our minds has been one of the keys to making that happen. God has to get the first and last word, and the only way we're going to recognize what He's saying is if we're familiar enough with Scripture to recognize His voice when we so desperately need Him to interrupt.

Finding God in the Messiness

When I got married, I didn't know how much I acted like an attorney when I was outside the office, even though Raquel said over and over again, "Stop talking to me like you're a lawyer."

"I'm not being a lawyer; I'm trying to *persuade* you to see my point of view. You just need to try to persuade me to see yours."

This approach to negotiation understandably exhausted Raquel, who found herself having to spar with me in order to avoid losing her "case," oftentimes over the most minor things. I just couldn't bear to be wrong or give in unless I had been sufficiently convinced otherwise.

The fact that I hung up my lawyer suit and voluntarily put myself on trial through those integrity interviews can only be attributed to the sovereign grace of God. He miraculously transplanted some humility that overrode my prideful propensities and gave me the willingness to raise my hand and say, "I'll sign up for that. Tell me how I need to grow." That didn't happen in a vacuum. Around that time, I was becoming more willing to open myself to God's examination, and it naturally manifested itself as a new expression of love in my marriage. Otherwise, it would've just been a deep dive into a journey of vain self-discovery.

If you're willing to allow God to use other people, Scripture, and/or personal examination to place you under His holy magnifying glass, beware. He's going to start to show you things that He wants to change in your life, and as you're filled with the Holy Spirit, you'll actually *want* to start making those changes—even seemingly minor ones.

Pay attention when you feel that desire to love a little stronger. The Holy Spirit is probably on the move *through you* (isn't that amazing?). Respond to Him by praying something like, "Lord, I do believe You're at work in me. I want to love my spouse just a little bit more today than I did yesterday. Please fill me up so that more of Your love overflows in my marriage."

You never know what might happen as you surrender more of your heart to loving your spouse. If you're like me, it might even end up turning your whole spiritual life upside down.

4

Prayer Pressure

THERE WAS A PARTICULAR MOMENT ONE NIGHT DURING OUR dating days that was a harbinger of things to come in our spiritual life as a couple. We had been dating for about a month, and we were on the phone when Raquel requested something that made me uncomfortable: She wanted to pray together.

There was something in Raquel's voice that made me feel that she expected something special, like this was my big moment to prove how spiritually mature I was. There was no way out, though. It would've been like dodging the first kiss. I took a deep breath.

"Sure, you go first," I said.

"I want *you* to go first," she said.

I didn't want to pray out loud with her. It's not that I had a problem with praying out loud. I did it all the time in church services and in small groups, but I rarely prayed one-on-one with a woman.

"All right," I said, girding my loins to pray and sensing that things were about to go terribly wrong. There was just this tinge of anticipation in her voice—the voice of a woman burning with desire for a spiritually romantic moment. But my relationship with God wasn't romantic. I just talked to Him, avoiding wordy supplications; I took a great deal of pride in my spontaneous, unplugged prayer life. Even so, I gritted my teeth and dove in.

"God," I said, "thanks for this moment. I don't know what's going on with Raquel and me at this stage, but I really like her and we're both Your children. Please direct us where we need to go. Otherwise, we're just floundering around, wasting each other's time. Please help us know what to do next because if this ends up being—um—a permanent relationship, we're going to have a lot to figure out. In Jesus' name, amen."

I waited in the silence, assuming Raquel was going to get started on her own prayer. She didn't. Instead, she asked me a question.

"Can you, like, *really* pray now?"

I was taken aback.

"What do you mean?" I asked defensively.

"I'm not trying to be rude," she said, "but I just think that if you're going to pray, you need to do it in a way that sounds more . . . meaningful."

I couldn't believe what she was saying.

"There's not some way you're supposed to pray, Raquel. You're supposed to talk to God like you'd talk to your dad. That's what I did, and I think God is OK with that. You can pray now if you want."

Thus she began to pray—*really* pray, apparently. I couldn't concentrate on whatever she was saying, though, because I was so distracted by the fact that she was, in effect, doing a demo prayer for me. I felt embarrassed by it, like she was trying to teach me how to sing a praise song properly in church. In the end, however, our prayers had at least one thing in common: the word *amen*, which I was grateful to hear.

Raquel and I kept praying together throughout dating and our engagement, but I generally stuck to my casual, nonchalant style—and that was every bit intentional. That's the way I had always connected with God in prayer. I knew I might have to change in some areas when I got married, but the last thing I was going to let Raquel do was tell me how to talk to God.

It wasn't all bad. We had a lot of bright spots in our premarital spiritual life. There were the honest, desperate prayers we offered at the end of our high-octane counseling sessions with our pastor, when we felt so emotionally spent that we couldn't help but let our guards down. Plus, as I mentioned before, we both repeatedly and earnestly asked God to be the center of attention at our wedding. And in the last month of our engagement, our defenses thawed and we began trusting God for a happier life after the vows.

So, to be fair, I think we got off to a decent start when it came to spiritual intimacy—at least we were trying. I just didn't anticipate how hard it would be to make any progress in that area after we tied the knot.

Prayer Drives

After Raquel and I got married, I knew I should want to be spiritually intimate with her, but I just didn't have the same appetite for it that she did. She wanted regular, intense, extended prayer, and she wanted us to read a passage of Scripture together regularly. Basically, she wanted me to take the lead when it came to the spiritual growth of our marriage. But I was too proud to do my job. Not surprisingly, my resistance found its way to other areas of our marriage.

I resented Raquel's to-do list. I didn't want her presuming to assign me any jobs whatsoever—washing dishes, getting the oil changed, or calling the cable company to ask about the bill, to name a few. And if I wanted to be the spiritual leader of my home, I would decide on my own to take that job. I was determined that my spiritual life was going to keep looking like it did before we got married: a close but unstructured relationship with God. I would be the one who decided if or when I felt like doing things like praying, reading my Bible, or any other spiritual disciplines. In other words, I was spiritually lazy, and I certainly wasn't going to have her ordering me off the couch.

Raquel noticed my resistance, and it only seemed to inspire her to push me harder. We would be eating dinner and she would mention that she wanted us to pray and read through a passage of Scripture before we went to bed. What was I supposed to say?

When we got in bed, I wouldn't mention our scheduled prayer time, hoping that she would forget. It never worked.

"Joshua," she would say with a hint of irritation in her voice, "you said we were going to pray and read the Bible together."

"Oh yeah—it's kind of late, though."

"Joshua, we never pray together. We have to make this a priority. Go ahead and pray."

Rather than pray, I would complain about her pushiness and she would complain about my unwilling attitude. Eventually, I would force out a prayer, which I seriously doubt got past the ceiling, and that was that. We didn't fare any better with trying to read the Bible together.

"Why don't you pick out a passage for us?" Raquel would prompt me.

"OK," I'd say, throwing my Bible open and picking a random passage from the Psalms or the Gospels. Raquel would critique my patent carelessness, and I would criticize her for having such a critical spirit. I just wanted to go back to my spontaneous, undisciplined spiritual life, but it was too late. I was married to a woman who wouldn't leave well enough alone, and that was going to turn out to be a very good thing.

A Difficult Trail to Follow

Over the course of our first three years of marriage, our prayer life began to change. While we still occasionally scrapped over when we would pray or how often we would do so, the tension gradually dissipated.

I can't point to a particular moment or season that changed our early prayer life. We just kept trying, and even at our fussiest, most immature moments, we never once threw up our hands and said, "Fine—let's just not pray at all." Prayer was never optional.

Our wobbly spiritual legs progressively grew stronger as we prayed together, and there were circumstances that strengthened them even more. That was especially the case when it came to Raquel's pregnancies. When those little lives began growing inside Raquel, we were determined from day one to cover them in prayer so that when they arrived, they would be as spiritually healthy as possible.

Night after night, I would place my hand over Raquel's womb, and we would pray and then sing Jesus songs together for the baby to hear. It didn't occur to me that we were having an intimate time of prayer and worship. We were just doing the only thing we could to help our children get a head start on being spiritually healthy.

There were also these unexpected, isolated moments when we would find ourselves experiencing spiritual intimacy that far exceeded our level of spiritual maturity as a couple. One night in particular stands out. We were at the Sunday evening church service when I went up to take communion at the kneeler. Usually, when I was waiting to take the bread and wine, I would pray for two things: physical healing that someone needed and reconciliation for strained relationships. That night, however, before I could pray as usual, I had another prayer dart into my thoughts. I wondered if it was something provoked by the Holy Spirit because it kept coming to me as I waited at the rail: "Please give Raquel grace when she goes through the fire."

When we got home, I shared the prayer with Raquel. She was troubled, wondering what it might mean. I didn't have any further clarity, but suddenly I felt a strong imperative for us to pray about it. We knelt beside the bed, and as I waited in the silence, I knew that the landscape around Raquel was about to be charred by hard, painful circumstances. But I prayed in faith that after the smoke cleared, she would remain standing, like a flower that miraculously survived the flames.

I had never prayed for Raquel with such fervency before, but it felt redemptive. I was taking care of her in a way that had once been a weakness. What I didn't realize—as I was praying for her— was that the fire was coming, and it would eventually take us both to a place of spiritual intimacy that we'd never been before.

Giving In

In our third year of marriage, we moved to Raleigh, North Carolina, in pursuit of my dream job. It was an intimidating step for us to uproot our family and leave Washington, but we encouraged ourselves by remembering God's assurance to Israel in Isaiah:

Fear not, for I have redeemed you; I have called you by name, you are mine. When you pass through the waters, I will be with you; and through the rivers, they shall not overwhelm you; when you walk through fire you shall not be burned, and the flame shall not consume you. (Isaiah 43:1–2 ESV)

The fire was already raging around Raquel by the time we moved to Raleigh. The move alone was hard, but we had a couple of needy toddlers in tow. Once we got established, Raquel didn't have any close friendships and was working through the fallout of her parents' recent divorce. Every day she felt trapped inside our house.

Around the time that Raquel was staying at home with the girls, she joined a contemplative prayer group that met once a month for three hours straight. I didn't know what they were doing—something about silent prayer, praying through the Scripture, and prayerfully listening to each other—but I didn't want anything to do with it.

Three hours was too long to pray, and I preferred talking to God while I was driving home from work anyway. Eventually, however, Raquel started suggesting that I get involved too. I politely resisted. It felt like those times when she had tried to arm-twist me into praying "meaningful" prayers. We had come a long way since then, and I didn't see any reason for us to take things in a different direction.

Raquel would try to get me to read the materials she brought home from her prayer gatherings, apparently thinking I would actually adopt some of the spiritual disciplines described in them. If I looked at them at all, I would just skim over them in bed and hand them back to her.

"Just go on one of their silent retreats," she urged. "They only last half a day."

"I can't take half a day off for a prayer retreat," I replied each time she mentioned it, but the truth was that I didn't want to. As a chronically extroverted person, a silent retreat sounded like torture.

It was my pride, oddly enough, that finally pushed me to attend one of the silent retreats. I was afraid that if I didn't go, Raquel would look down on me as her spiritually immature husband. This was my chance to prove I was just as spiritual as she was. So I decided I was going to go on that retreat, and I was going to like it, whether I wanted to or not.

It's hard to explain what happened in the three hours of the retreat. There was this calming combination of silent prayer, listening quietly to the same Scripture passage being read repeatedly, and even eating soup and sandwiches together without talking. To my surprise, it was wonderful.

For the first time in years, I became aware of how much racket was going on in my head, and after an hour or so, I experienced the sweet heaviness of God's presence as I prayed without words. I didn't realize how desperately my soul needed to accept Jesus' invitation to His disciples: "Come with me by yourselves to a quiet place and get some rest" (Mark 6:31). I also didn't realize how much my marriage needed that rest as well.

After the retreat, Raquel successfully got me to participate in her monthly prayer group, which was similar to what the silent retreat had been like. I actually began to look forward to our monthly meetings, and when we eventually moved back to DC, leaving that group behind was one of our greatest losses. Even so, we discovered that the group didn't have to end—we still had each other.

Although Raquel and I didn't start a formal routine of three-hour prayer retreats in the living room or anything, we did start incorporating some of the most basic practices into our prayer times together. There are a few of them, in particular, that have enriched our prayer life in ways I never imagined back when Raquel and I were arguing over what it meant to "really pray." When we combined those together with the ways we were already praying before, it resulted in spiritual intimacy that, with just a little bit of effort, any couple can experience.

The Baseline

I hope you and your spouse find it easy to spend time praying together, but if you're like Raquel and I were in our earlier years of marriage, it may not be your strong suit. You may even be like some Christian couples I know who hardly pray together at all. If so, don't give up hope. There's at least a baseline of spiritual activity that you can aim for.

The most important starting point for a great prayer life as a couple is to pray together regularly. Pray quick prayers. Pray when you're too tired to do it. Pray when you're mad at each other (*especially* when you're mad at each other). Pray before you eat and when you go to sleep. Pray long prayers or short prayers—it's not words or the length of the prayer that matters; it's the fact that the two of you are directing your needs to your heavenly Father.

Don't feel bad if your prayer life feels bland. When Raquel and I began our journey of learning to pray together, the vast majority of the time I was just saying words and hoping that doing so counted for something to God. We were consistently praying before we ate, praying before we went to sleep, and asking God for little things like helping us find our keys. Sometimes we had sweet times of prayer, but those felt like the exception. And you know what? That was OK—at least we were doing something.

Raquel and I still have times when we feel like we're not getting anywhere with our prayers. In those times, I just remind myself that we love to hear from our kids, even when they're not being particularly impressive, and I'm sure God feels the same way about His children.

Just the other night, for example, we were lying in bed in the dark and Raquel asked me to pray about something that's weighing on our hearts right now. I was tired, but I sincerely prayed about it, and when I wrapped up, I said, "Do you want to pray now, Raquel?"

"I'm barely awake," Raquel replied in a whisper. At least we had prayed. I have no doubt God answered that prayer and that He has answered many others like it. For some, the main problem is just figuring out what to say. Praying can feel awkward and forced. If this is your experience, don't worry; there's a prayer practice that's just right for you: silence.

Getting Quiet

If you think back to where Raquel and I started having tension in our prayer life, it was all about the words I was saying. I felt like I was being edited by Raquel as I spoke. Silence in prayer brought some relief to that tension.

When Raquel first introduced silence to our prayer time, I struggled. It was one thing to be silent in the middle of a forest at a retreat, but it was a different story when Raquel and I were lying in bed and she suggested it.

"Here we go," I would think, but I had no good reason to refuse. So I would sigh, get quiet, and stare forward. Distraction and preoccupation zipped through my head like cars on the freeway, and I would just wait for the quiet to end.

As Raquel kept gently insisting that we regularly spend time in prayerful silence, it started to become a regular part of our prayer life. Occasionally, there were moments when the silence felt like a gift. It was calming—if only for a couple of minutes—to stop hearing the noise in my head and open up to whatever God wanted to do in my heart.

Many times when Raquel and I had prayed together in the past, my prayers were all words. Sure, I was trying, which was a start, but I don't even think I was praying a lot of the time. I was starting prayers with God's name and from that point forward, I was just giving Raquel a pep talk or talking out loud about how I thought God should handle this or that situation. Silence changed that. It slowed things down and reminded me that praying with

Raquel isn't all about the words we hear each other say. It's about us getting quiet and listening to what God has to say to us.

Just a couple of prayerful minutes without words helps us see that prayer isn't just an exercise of our mouths; it's a reverent posture of our hearts, and Scripture reminds us of its value. Psalm 62:1 says, "For God alone my soul waits in silence; from him comes my salvation" (ESV). Lamentations 3:26 states, "It is good that one should wait quietly for the salvation of the LORD" (ESV). And many of us are familiar with Psalm 46:10: "Be still, and know that I am God."

Raquel and I have never heard God speak audibly. Many times, however, when we're praying together silently, the Holy Spirit's inaudible voice goes deep, deep down into our hearts and reminds us of something we often forget in the racket of day-to-day life: *He's here with us.* That's it, but what could be more comforting?

Simply being aware of His presence sheds a new light on all our preoccupations and concerns. They shrink down to size as He is magnified in the stillness. Quiet awareness gets our words out of the way and puts Him at the center of our attention. That's something we desperately need in our marriage, which is often pulled in every direction but heavenward.

Praying Through the Word

While praying in silence is all well and good for some people, there are others who (like me) start to get fidgety if it goes on aimlessly. We need some structure, something to help us direct our thoughts toward God. There's nothing better than God's thoughts to help us do that.

Sometimes Raquel and I pray through Scripture together, and it is one of the most powerful ways we use prayer to connect with God and each other (this is also called *lectio divina*). This is basically how it works:

1. We take a passage of Scripture and one of us reads it out loud.
2. We pause for a couple of minutes and let the passage sink in. In the silence, we wait to see if the Holy Spirit draws our attention to any particular part of the passage.
3. We read it out loud again.
4. We pause for a couple more minutes, during which we pray something like, "God, how are You using the Word to speak to us about our current circumstances?"
5. We read the passage one more time and silently ask God, "What's Your invitation to us right now?" In the quiet, we wait for Him to make that clear. Sometimes He does; sometimes He doesn't. The most important thing is that we draw near to Him.

Usually, these moments of praying through the Scripture are opportunities to get still and let the Lord bring His Word alive. We slowly chew on the Word and savor it, rather than chomping down a chapter and swallowing it without even tasting it. The experience helps us release the distractions that compete for our attention and give the Holy Spirit room to fill the silence with His wisdom.

In one instance, slowing down and digesting Scripture brought comfort to Raquel and me in the midst of a hard decision. As I mentioned earlier in the chapter, Isaiah 43:1–2 was a passage we held on to when we decided to uproot our lives and move to North Carolina. It had gotten into our heads because our church sang the words in a song that was appropriately titled "Isaiah 43."

We knew it would be difficult to leave everything behind and go to another city, but we sensed God's call. And as we read the passage again and again that night, we were reminded of God's faithfulness. He was extending an invitation to us: "If I called you to leave Washington, I will make a way for you. I'm faithful to those I call My own. You can trust Me." With restful hearts, we released our journey to Him, counting on Him to lead us.

I'm sure that passage would've been meaningful to us if we had simply read it through once and said a prayer. But after taking bite after bite of that same passage and savoring each morsel, we started digesting the reality that God's faithfulness was true for us and believing that we could trust Him as we moved forward into the unknown. When I look back at that moment, I can still see where I was sitting and feel the same assurance that I did when we meditated on Isaiah 43. His Word came alive in us because we slowed down and gave it time to make His love clear to us.

To you and your spouse, I say this: Give prayerful reading of

Scripture a shot, even if it feels awkward. You may be surprised to discover the pleasure that comes when you "taste and see that the LORD is good" (Psalm 34:8 ESV).

Prayers of Examination

A while back, Raquel and I hosted a surprise party for our friend Eric. As we all waited for him to show up, the tension mounted. Finally, he came to our front door. He opened the door, we all yelled, "Surprise!" and he doubled over in laughter and kept saying, "I can't believe you did this!"

I'm already an excitable extrovert, and from that point forward at the party, I was on an emotional high. I was loud and boisterous, telling lots of stories and carrying on long conversations. There were also a few moments when I poked fun at Eric in good humor and got some laughs out of it.

The next day, Raquel suggested that we look back on the previous day and do a prayer of examination (otherwise known as a Prayer of Examen, which Ignatius of Loyola developed over five hundred years ago). Basically, during these prayers, you bring yourself before God, acknowledge His presence and His love for you, and review your day like you're watching a movie. It's a way of issuing this invitation from Psalm 139:23–24: "Search me, God, and know my heart. . . . See if there is any offensive way in me, and lead me in the way everlasting." It's also an opportunity for the Lord to bring to remembrance encouraging ways that He was at work in your day.

When you're doing a prayer of self-examination, you can ask yourself questions like the following:

- What was I most grateful for today?
- What was I least grateful for?
- Did I feel myself walking in step with the Lord at any point?
- Did I resist God at any point?
- Was there anything that was particularly life-giving?
- Was there anything that drained me?
- Where did I give and receive the most love?
- Where did I give and receive the least love?

A Prayer of Examen, as Richard Foster explains in his classic book *Prayer*, offers "the priceless grace of self-knowledge." It isn't, however, an exercise in *self-absorption*. That's useless, and it's not the point of practicing the Prayer of Examen at all. The point is to retrace our footsteps with the Lord, identify the way we live each day, and offer Him "who we are—not who we want to be," as Foster says. God then takes our offering and, in showing us who we really are, allows us to become more aware of how He is present and working in our lives.

I've practiced the Prayer of Examen in my personal prayer time, but just as often, Raquel and I have used it together. For example, as I prayerfully reflected on Eric's surprise party, which had seemed like a flawless event after we said goodbye to him, it began to emerge as a more complicated experience. Yes, there were many moments in which I noticed God at work—the unexpected word of encouragement from a child who was there, a rich conversation with Eric, and a spontaneous moment of prayer with a friend. But there was another side of the experience that I didn't notice at the time. My "poking fun" at Eric bordered on putting him down at times. I listened very little and talked quite a lot. I occasionally bragged about some recent successes.

"Raquel," I said after we'd completed the Prayer of Examen, "the party was really good, but it could've been better. I was a jerk some of the time—especially toward Eric. It's like I was trying to be the big dog and put him in his place. I also dominated conversations with others too much." As a result of this revelation, I was able to confess my sin to Raquel, and later on I apologized to Eric. It all started with being willing to join Raquel in coming to the Lord with every moment of my life. And it reminded me that prayerful examination is one of the most powerful ways you can experience vulnerability with God and your spouse.

Gratitude

One morning, Raquel woke up and was irritable from the time she got out of bed. She kept focusing on all the negative things that were happening around her. I tried to remind her of the many positive things going on in our lives, but she just kept processing her disappointments. After a while I felt like we had reached the point where her feelings had been sufficiently validated and her negativity needed to be redirected.

"You know," I said, "the more you talk about all this negative stuff, the bigger it's going to become in your mind."

Raquel crossed her arms and sighed.

"It just feels like everything is going wrong right now." Then she named off a handful of legitimately frustrating things.

"Raquel, I want to do something."

She knew what was coming because I've done it so many times before. Whenever she starts focusing on the negative, I ask her to think of five things she's grateful for. This time, I took it to the next level and asked her to think of fifteen things she was thankful for.

"Fifteen?" she said. "I can't think of fifteen things."

"Oh, come on," I said, smiling. "That's easy. Number one is me."

Raquel took me up on my gratitude challenge and, one by one, named off things she was thankful for. She started struggling at number eleven but managed to press forward when she got creative and started thanking God for things like cookies and air-conditioning. By the end, we were laughing together. She said that it felt like a negative cloud that was surrounding her had lifted and that her body even started feeling different as the tension dissipated and she began to feel more relaxed.

Moments of gratitude like that are also a big part of our prayer life as a couple. If it's late at night and we're tired but we still want to pray, we'll tell God one thing we're grateful for and one thing we need. There are other times when we'll be praying together and we'll just praise God for thing after thing that He's done for us. It's so life-giving and freeing for us to release the burdens we carry and lift up praise in a sound of joyful obedience to God's Word, which includes dozens of encouragements to be thankful.

The next time you and your spouse pray, take a break from asking God for things and just thank Him for what He's already given you. Do something as simple as naming five things you're grateful for and then tell Him how good He is. Or don't even try to count: Go back and forth, and just keep going. Get about the business of prayerful joy as a couple and you may be surprised by the joy it brings into your relationship with God and each other.

Finding God in the Messiness

I've prayed all my life in church, small groups, and with friends, but I never really considered myself a man of prayer.

When I prayed, sometimes I felt God's presence strongly or was certain that He would answer. Most of the time, though, I felt like I was just talking out loud while I was drifting off to sleep or driving through traffic. Then I got married.

I had always looked down on those guys whose wives had to shove them from behind to get them to engage with their faith. When I married Raquel, it turned out that, in my own way, I was one of those guys. I married a righteous woman of prayer, and she wasn't putting up with my spiritual passivity. She wanted me to pray—*really* pray.

As Raquel has persistently nudged me into a deeper walk with the Lord, I've grown to love drawing close to God in a more struc-tured way and I've been taking my role as a spiritual leader in my home more seriously. For example, I recently went into the room of my two-year-old son, Isaiah, and prayed for him. When I said, "Amen," he said, "Good night, Daddy," and then he said, "Good night, Jesus." He's already learning how to pray.

In another recent example, I went into my girls' bedroom and the three of us got down on our knees in the dark. We each told God one thing we were grateful for, one thing we needed, and one thing someone else needed. After that, I went to my bedroom, where I found Raquel downcast over a host of hard things that have happened recently. At my insistence, we prayed through a passage of Scripture together.

If Raquel weren't such a woman of prayer, I would still be willing to lead prayer in our home, but it would just be spontaneous and haphazard, like my spiritual life before Raquel came into it. She called me to be a leader, but she had to take the lead to get me there. Raquel showed me that prayer isn't an accessory to our family's daily life—it's at the heart of it.

I think it must bring a smile to God's face to see Raquel and me, His children, come before His throne, awkwardly holding hands and saying, "Hi, Dad." He made us for this—for oneness. Physical intimacy unifies bodies, but spiritual intimacy unifies souls.

James 4:8 contains a beautiful promise: "Draw near to God and He will draw near to you" (NKJV). When you draw near to God as a couple, He draws near to your relationship; and with that kind of love and intimacy, you can't help but have a stronger marriage.

5

Grace and
the In-Laws

THE FIRST TIME RAQUEL MET MY DAD WAS AT OUR WEDDING
rehearsal. I would've liked for her to have met him before then,
just to help prepare her for what he was like. But he lived in
another state and our engagement was so short that all I could
offer were my descriptions of him, none of which did him justice.

"My dad is like—I don't know—this truck driver preacher
who talks to everyone he meets. He's kind of eccentric."

When Raquel finally met my dad at the wedding rehearsal,
his peculiarity became more evident. She saw a man who was
the shadow of who he had once been. His quirky personality

was the same, but years of driving trucks and smoking cigarettes, coupled with mostly untreated type 2 diabetes, had worn his body down. He was overweight, he walked with a limp, and he had deep wrinkles on his face. They couldn't hide his electric blue eyes though. They were as lit up with childlike love and affection as they ever had been.

My mom, a blue-eyed beauty with salt-and-pepper hair, had been divorced from Dad for fourteen years when I got married, and she was a striking contrast to him: taller, nicely dressed, still looking younger than her age. At least Dad wore a suit to the rehearsal dinner, even if it looked like an oversized one that he had picked up from the thrift store. I'm sure he knew that it would mean a lot to me.

Mom was hosting the dinner at a nice restaurant, and it involved a number of short speeches. She didn't want it to drag on, so she specifically requested that each person speak no more than two to four minutes. Everyone complied with her directive except Dad, of course. His speech was a long, peculiar diatribe in which he eventually began drawing an analogy between a jet and me.

"People tried to tell Josh to get started dating and just settle on some girl, but then he met Raquel. And in my mind, I saw him go *up, up, up* and begin *soaring* in the air like a . . ." Then Dad added sound effects with a loud shush and moved his hand up like he was playing charades and the answer was "jet."

"Then," he said, "as the jet went past those clouds—"

Before Dad could reach the climax of his story, Mom stood up and started clapping, effectively winding down his speech.

Everyone else joined her in an uncertain slow clap, no doubt grateful that Dad's speech had come to a close before he could keep going. God only knows what he might have said if Mom hadn't interrupted.

Before the dinner was over, Dad took Raquel aside and told her what a beautiful woman she was and how God had chosen her to be my wife and how He had also chosen her to be his daughter.

"I'm your daddy too," he said with a warm smile. "Once you marry Joshua, you're my little girl." And then he kept lavishing praise upon praise as she smiled politely. Dad didn't notice, but she was looking down and edging away a little bit. It was understandable. Within the span of five hours, this unusual man in a secondhand suit had zoomed from "hello" to "I am your father." In short, Raquel quickly learned she would probably have to exercise a lot of grace toward my dad.

Yellow Light, Green Light

My relationship with Raquel's dad, Charlie, got off to a better start than hers did with my dad.

Three months after first saying hello to Raquel at a party, I called Charlie to ask if we could meet to "talk about my relationship with Raquel."

"Say no more," he replied. "I understand."

Before meeting with Charlie, I had gotten on my knees and admitted to the Lord that I wasn't sure if I was doing the right thing. "Father," I prayed, "I've always hoped that You'd give me some sort of sign when it became the right decision to move forward with marriage, but You haven't. So I just want You to know that—with or without a sign—I'm choosing Raquel because she's the woman I want. Please give me Your blessing."

About an hour later, I met with Raquel's dad for breakfast at a little diner in Delaware. We started with small talk that lasted for about five minutes. Then he asked the question: "So what did you want to talk about?"

I looked down at my omelet and blurted out, "I'd like to have permission to marry your daughter."

"Whoa, whoa, whoa," he said. "You told me you wanted to talk about your relationship with Raquel."

"Well, I did."

Thus began an exhausting ninety-minute conversation in which we went round and round discussing whether this was the right time for Raquel and me to get married. Charlie raised legitimate concerns—for example, Raquel was starting an MBA program and working full-time. I tried to address them the best I could, but we kept retreading the same ground, which always led him to the same conclusion: "I'm not at a total green light right now, but it's not a red light either. It's yellowish."

Finally, Charlie asked a question that turned the conversation upside down. "When were you planning on doing this?"

"I'd like to ask her to marry me on her birthday so she won't see it coming," I explained. I had given this plan some thought.

Charlie looked down, pausing, as I waited for him to respond. When he looked up, his eyes were filled with tears.

"You have my permission," he said. "It's a green light—100

percent. God showed Raquel's mother and me that this was going to happen."

After composing himself, he said, "A year ago, Raquel's mother was awake and had a vision. She saw a small birthday cake with one candle on it and there was an engagement ring around the base of the candle. We wondered what it meant. Well, now we know. That engagement ring on the birthday cake belongs to Raquel."

I was in awe. It would've been enough for me if my future father-in-law had said yes, but I got more than that: My Father in heaven stepped in and said yes along with Charlie.

White Lights and Puerto Rican Stuffing

Despite the supernatural experience with Raquel's parents, which bonded me to them early on, little things reminded me that it was going to take some time for me to feel like a part of the family. It all started with the holidays.

Raquel grew up with Christmas trees that were only decorated with white lights, and she is of the opinion that colored lights just don't look as good on a Christmas tree. I was not aware of this when we married.

"I've always had colored Christmas lights on the tree," I told Raquel after she declared that our tree would only have white lights.

"Well, you're not going to have colored Christmas lights on the tree anymore," she replied. "I'm in charge of home décor, and the Christmas tree definitely falls into that category."

I repeatedly asked Raquel to change her mind, but it was a losing battle. She dismissed the request every time I suggested it and would take the colored lights out of the shopping cart at Walmart whenever I tried to put them in there. I slumped my shoulders and shook my head. At least we still gave gifts.

I could make it without colored lights at Christmas, but Thanksgiving was a whole other issue. Thanksgiving was the day reserved for my family's annual reunion. I had never missed it until the second year of our marriage when we spent it with Raquel's family instead.

I was so downtrodden as Raquel and I rode up to Delaware together with her sister in the car. As we drove through Baltimore, I got a call from my cousin Elizabeth, who's like a sister to me. She was in tears that I wouldn't be joining them, and before long, I had a lump in my throat. This was the first Thanksgiving we had been apart since we were kids.

"I love you so much," I said and got off the phone, sitting in silence until my sister-in-law spoke up after a couple of minutes.

"I'm sorry you're away from your family, but it's like you don't want to be with your new family this Thanksgiving."

I felt like saying, "I sure don't." But, in a moment of extraordinary self-control, I restrained myself. My sister-in-law wanted me to integrate into my new family, but I didn't care. I wanted things the way they used to be, especially when it came to my beloved dressing.

Dressing—not to be confused with stuffing—is a Southern, carbohydrate-laden holiday delicacy. There are various iterations of the recipe, but my mom uses the best combination: shredded chicken, eggs, corn bread, sage, and enough white bread to feed the University of Southern Mississippi football team. Thanksgiving isn't a holiday without it—at least I thought it wasn't until I experienced Thanksgiving with Raquel and her parents.

"We're having my mom's stuffing with Thanksgiving dinner," Raquel said.

I sighed. I wasn't looking forward to eating someone's variation of the old bread crumb–based Stove Top stuffing, but I had eaten Stove Top before, and although it wasn't dressing, I could live with it as long as I could dowse it in gravy. As it turned out, however, we were having Puerto Rican "stuffing," an interesting combination of ground beef, green olives, spices, and plantains instead of bread.

"How is that supposed to be stuffing?" I whispered to Raquel as we prepared to eat Thanksgiving dinner with her family. "What in the world would you 'stuff' with it?"

"Stop being so picky, Joshua," Raquel answered. "She found the recipe in a Puerto Rican newspaper years ago. It's wonderful."

I didn't make a big deal about it, but it just didn't taste like Thanksgiving to me at all. It tasted like a whole new life that was going to require some adjustment.

Finding the Connection Point

For all the changes I would eventually experience in being related to Raquel's family, one of the great gifts has been having in-laws who constantly lift us up in prayer. It's a way of life for them, and it's one of the things that connected us from the start. If either of Raquel's parents or her sister were in our home and we wanted to have a prayer meeting, we could rest assured that we would be bowing our heads with people who want to meet with Jesus. Some people could only dream of having in-laws like that.

In addition to being a woman of prayer, my mom is also an artist. Her home is overflowing with a cornucopia of fabrics that she uses to make masterpiece quilts. Several of those treasured quilts, which take hours to finish, have made it to our home, along with many other crafts she designs for our family (among our favorites are her indestructible crocheted pot holders). I don't know any couple whose kids get priceless gifts like homemade quilts from their grandmother, but in our house, it's our greatest connection point to her, especially because she lives a thousand miles away from us.

Maybe you struggle to connect with your in-laws, who may not be interested in prayer meetings and don't send homemade crafts in the mail. But unless your in-law is a toxic person whom you need to stay away from entirely, there's some connection point to be made, and it's really a matter of having the humility to find it. Does your mother-in-law like to watch TV shows that aren't up your alley? Park it on the couch next to her and let yourself enjoy watching something just because she does. Does your father-in-law start mowing the lawn every time you and your kids show up? Come wearing an old T-shirt next time and pull some weeds. Maybe your in-laws won't be appreciative, but there's a beauty in your willingness to try.

Making a genuine effort to connect to your in-laws is actually an imitation of Christ. He's the One who entered into our space and became like us so that He could do whatever it took to be close to us. Imagine the power of doing the same on a miniscule level with your spouse's family. I don't have to imagine what that would be like—not because I've excelled in this area, but because I saw my wife set aside her discomfort and love my dad in a way that will undoubtedly live on in eternity.

Honor Thy Father-in-Law

Over the years, Raquel treated Dad far differently from how other people treated him. When he came to visit, she gave him a hug and overlooked the scent of mildew in his flannel shirt and the holes in his sweatpants. She talked with him like the intellectual giant he was rather than withdrawing a safe distance from him to avoid his tendency to ramble on about the spiritual insights he had gained over the years. The only woman whom I'd ever seen treat Dad that way was my mom, back in the early days of their marriage. And now my wife was respecting and affirming him.

After Raquel's first experience with Dad at the rehearsal dinner, I assured her that he had mellowed out in the years since he and Mom had divorced, and he wasn't as eccentric as he had been before. I think it was helpful for her to know that, but regardless of whether he had mellowed, he was still a wild stallion.

Dad would intentionally create awkward moments in public that would embarrass my brother, Caleb, and me as well as our wives. He wasn't afraid to take his humor too far—way too far. A perfect example was the time our families went with him to a playground and he squeezed onto a plastic swing that was intended for small children. Dad literally started acting like he was six years old, barely moving but pretending like he was on a roller coaster. We got a little embarrassed at first, but we soon felt mortified when a child and her dad came up and began waiting for a turn on the swing. We began imploring him to get off the swing, but he kept going.

"Yay! This is fun!" Dad hollered with glee as we looked on in horror. My kids, who adored him, thought antics like this were brilliant. He may have been seen as childish by some, but thanks to his willingness to be childlike, no other adult has ever come close to matching his ability to get on our kids' level and play with them.

Another thing about Dad was that he had a deep understanding of Scripture and theology that few could match. He would approach strangers and wrangle them into long conversations about the Bible. The Lord deeply touched some people who appeared to enjoy the exchange (assuming they could get a word in); others got exhausted and would try to wrap things up. In these cases, Dad was likely to take them by the hand and engage in a long, awkward prayer before finally letting them go.

With the burden of Dad's lack of reserve came a benefit that made it all worth it: He never restrained himself from affirming Raquel, the kids, or me. I wasn't surprised. I had been on the receiving end of his affirmation my whole life, but his affirmation of Raquel was especially meaningful to me.

Dad praised his "daughter": He marveled at her intellect and the depth of her spirituality; he affirmed her beauty in a fatherly way. He asked for her opinion, listened intently when she shared her thoughts, and, with a tone of genuine conviction, affirmed her wisdom. It meant everything to me that Dad noticed and appreciated the goodness of the woman I loved so dearly, and it meant even more that Raquel saw the goodness and beauty in him.

Raquel didn't push the phone away when I would suddenly hand it to her and say, "Dad wants to talk to you." She took the time to listen and chat with him for a few minutes, which was probably the highlight of Dad's week. Raquel wanted him to be with us on holidays, and she didn't ask how much I was going to spend when I took Dad to Walmart to buy him a new wardrobe. She served him meals with a smile on her face, joined me in singing duets to him, and learned to laugh at his odd sense of humor. (For example, he would initiate the "Laughing Game," where we all sat around in a circle and, one by one, did the best laugh we could muster—eventually everyone started laughing out of control).

Little by little, Raquel's first impression of my father became a thing of the past. She would tell others, "Once you get to know David, you can't help but love him." Her willingness to love my dad like that only made me love her more.

Scripture commands us to honor our father and mother, "which is the first commandment with a promise—'so that it may go well with you and that you may enjoy long life on the earth'" (Ephesians 6:2–3). Ever since I was a child, I've wondered whether there is literal truth to the verse. No matter the meaning, here's what I do know: Whatever it guarantees belongs to Raquel.

One of the Great Secrets

Raquel's love simplified an in-law situation that could have been more complex. She gradually let herself see Dad's good qualities and focused less on his unattractive ones (something she has also done with me). I didn't realize it at the time, but that moment at the rehearsal dinner was significant. Dad was making her uncomfortable, no doubt, but she didn't pronounce judgment. She gave him a shot.

Raquel wasn't sure if Dad was safe at first, but she invited him in anyway. She served him and took time to listen to him. She noticed the way he loved our children and she literally embraced him, again and again. I think that was the key to the way she came to love him. Like C. S. Lewis said in *Mere Christianity*, "Do not waste time bothering whether you 'love' your neighbor; act as if you did. As soon as we do this we find one of the great secrets. When you are behaving as if you loved someone, you will presently come to love him."

The harder thing is to know how to honor an in-law who is emotionally unsafe. Maybe your in-law lies to you, manipulates you, mistreats your kids, or puts your spouse down. The absolute worst is an in-law who pulls you and your spouse apart. It can be subtle, like when you're the only one who gets invited to a family get-together. Or it can be more blatant, like when your in-law tries to turn the two of you against each other through gossip or criticism. I wish this kind of thing were uncommon, but if I shared with you some of the harrowing accounts of my friends, sadly you probably wouldn't be surprised.

On a personal level, I can tell you this: I love my dad, but if he had been emotionally unsafe, my family would've had a very limited relationship with him. I don't believe there's anything wrong with that. Our first responsibility is to our spouse and kids, and if an in-law consistently mistreats one of us, the most honorable thing we can do is to pray that God keeps our hearts tender toward that person and gives him or her the grace to change. Honoring a parent doesn't mean that you have to submit to abuse. In fact, when it comes to in-laws who desire to control you, remind yourself that you actually don't have to submit to them and neither does your spouse. "Therefore shall a man leave his father and his mother, and shall cleave unto his wife: and they shall be one flesh" (Genesis 2:24 KJV).

No matter what approach you take to your in-laws, I think the most important thing is to set your heart on loving them as aggressively as you can. And as you do that, pay attention to those feelings you have when you get around them or even think about them. Take a long look at what's inside and see what God shows you about your heart. Perhaps in dealing with a difficult in-law, the Holy Spirit may be reminding you that "a person's wisdom yields patience; it is to one's glory to overlook an offense" (Proverbs 19:11).

Whatever the Lord shows you about your heart toward your in-laws, it stands as an invitation to pray, "Lord, reveal to me whether I'm loving my in-laws the best way that I can, and help me make the right decisions about what that looks like." The answer to that prayer will never be an easy one, but whatever God calls you to do will most certainly involve you and your spouse doing it in unity.

The Walls Come Down

One week before our second child was born, my in-laws separated. Although we tried to stay focused on the joy of new life in our family, we couldn't ignore their breakup. We had just attended a wedding with them that same month, and now they weren't even coming to the hospital together.

After Raquel's dad met his new granddaughter, we went to a fast-food restaurant together, where I began proposing strategies for him to reconcile with my mother-in-law.

"Please don't do this," I said. "If you divorce, my kids won't have a set of grandparents who are still together."

In the coming days, I called my father-in-law repeatedly, trying to figure out some way I could help hold things together. Raquel wanted her parents to go to counseling and bring their church into the crisis. What we wanted didn't matter. Within five months, the papers were signed and it was officially over. All that was left was for Raquel and me to process it together.

We were both emotionally disoriented. I was reliving my parents' divorce, and Raquel was spiraling downward into anxiety. This was compounded by the fact that we had recently moved to another state, where she felt lonely and disconnected from other people. Her isolation gave her too much time to think about her parents' separation, and without any opportunity to flesh it out with her parents in person, she decided to see a Christian counselor. Those sessions, combined with Raquel's journey into contemplative prayer, helped her begin the process of healing. Even so, neither of us realized how much more work God needed to do in us.

The day we knew Raquel's parents' marriage was truly over was when Raquel's dad called to tell me he was getting remarried. The woman, who was gracious and welcoming from the beginning, made a genuine effort to get to know us, but it was hard to reciprocate at first. We had still been living with the irrational hope that Raquel's parents would reconcile. A few weeks after Charlie announced his engagement, he got remarried and we entered a new chapter as a family—one that was unfamiliar to Raquel and all too familiar to me. We had to accept the fact that, whether we liked it or not, the changes with her parents' lives were impacting ours.

Sometimes, as in our case, your in-laws are good people whose problems can't be avoided. When their struggles start expanding further and further into your space, it's hard to maintain your independence from those issues, whether it's marital conflict, financial struggles, health problems, or conflicts with other family members. All that stress can make its way into your home and generate unwanted anxiety for your family. Don't blame the in-laws, though. It's your responsibility to do your best to guard the door of your home, to keep your family from becoming enmeshed with your in-laws' burdens.

With Raquel's parents' divorce, I should've completely stepped away from the situation. There was nothing we could do to turn things around, and it wasn't our job anyway. We had the advantage of living 150 miles away from them, so the lack of physical proximity would've made it easier to create emotional distance from what was going on. But unfortunately, we only recognized our need to maintain a healthy distance long after we were already emotionally tangled in their personal issues.

Whenever you put boundaries in place and start to disentangle yourself from your in-laws' burdens—burdens that you were not meant to carry—notice what kinds of feelings come to the surface. Pay attention to them and ask God to give you insight into what's going on. Then be prepared for the fact that He may want you to release their problems to Him, which may not come naturally, especially if you have a history of getting involved with their issues. It really comes down to the same boundary that you need to raise with an unsafe in-law: "leaving and cleaving" and letting God take care of others' needs.

Finding God in the Messiness

Our identities are tied up, to some degree, with our families. We share names, years of history, and baggage that everyone would rather forget. While some people may have the gift of being able to take pride in their roots, those roots are complicated for many others. Family histories can make you feel unworthy and ashamed (in my case, I was actually ashamed of my last name for years).

I can tell you, based on personal experience, that your willingness to esteem your spouse's family can have a powerful impact. Your in-laws are a part of your spouse. If you reject and/or speak ill of your spouse's family, you reject a part of your spouse. When you do your best to accept your spouse's family or, at the very least, speak as well of them as you can, you have effectively accepted a part of your spouse. It's another way of showing God's love to say, "I see you, all of you, and I choose to love all of that too." There's no better example of that than the way Raquel related to my dad.

When I was growing up, a lot of people put Dad down to my face—including family members on both sides of my family. What they didn't realize is that they were talking about a significant part of me—the man who gave me half of my DNA and two-thirds of my name (we share the same middle and last names). To put him down was to put me down, which is why it was so honoring and redemptive for Raquel to esteem him. In doing so, she was restoring his honor and mine, and she did so until the very end of his life.

In the last year Dad was alive, he began to succumb to his years-long battle with congestive heart failure and diabetes. He was admitted to the ICU three times before the summer of that year. I eventually flew to Arkansas to help him get his life together. I thought I had succeeded.

With the help of my brother, I helped Dad get a new apartment, got a decent cell phone for him, found a nice wheelchair at a pawn shop, and arranged home health-care visits with a local agency. My cousin Elizabeth, who lived in the same town as Dad, also coordinated a fund-raising effort and managed to get his apartment fully furnished and decorated nicely within a week. Raquel even provided some budget coaching to Dad, and he promised to follow her instructions. He didn't get a chance.

Four months after we helped Dad get his life together, he was lying in a hospital, barely clinging to life. It was Christmastime. I didn't know how long Dad would live, but I knew for certain that he wouldn't see the following Christmas.

On Christmas night, five days before Dad died, Raquel and I called him in the hospital and talked to him on speakerphone for about ten minutes. Having a conversation was difficult because his breathing was so labored.

"Hey, Dad," I said, "Raquel and I are going to sing to you."

I looked at her and mouthed the words, "Silent Night."

I fought off the lump in my throat as we sung the line "Sleep in heavenly peace, sleep in heavenly peace."

It was quiet for a moment after we finished, and then Dad said, "It's glorious. It's just glorious."

I don't know exactly what my dad was talking about when he said, "It's glorious." His voice trailed off after that. But knowing him, he was probably talking about the fact that I chose Raquel to be my wife. And if he'd had enough breath in his lungs, I'll bet he would've said the same thing he had told Raquel many times over: "You know, people tried to pressure Josh into getting married to just any girl, but he wouldn't do it—he waited for *you*. And in that moment, he was like a jet, going *up, up, up*—soaring into the sky. That's where he found you, and the two of you just flew and flew up in the clouds together."

6

Naked and Ashamed

WHEN I WAS IN HIGH SCHOOL, I WAS THE SKINNY KID WHO would spend hours on the phone with popular girls only to find out that they were actually interested in the jocks who could use the f-word as a noun, adjective, and verb all in one sentence.

I got picked on a lot by those popular guys, and it was in the worst way a teenage boy can be picked on: I got called "queer" on a weekly basis. It crushed me. The gist of their insults—that I didn't have what it took to please a woman—invaded my psyche and created a great deal of insecurity. That insecurity followed me into adulthood until that rainy night in May when Raquel walked into the famous hat party, I said hello, and everything changed.

We started dating and, in little time, it became clear that my attraction toward her was mutual. When we went to a wedding on our fifth date, we were slowly dancing to the Norah Jones song "Come Away with Me" during the reception. I was getting mentally intoxicated by being close to her; finally, I worked up the nerve to kiss her for the first time.

When I pulled away, I took a deep breath and said, "I don't think a kiss can get any better than that." But as I found out on our honeymoon eight months later, it could get better—much better.

Figuring It Out

One time when I was in college, my friend Colby and I were talking about how much we looked forward to having sex when we got married.

"You know," he said, "just because two people are married doesn't mean they're going to enjoy sex."

I furrowed my brow. It couldn't be true.

"Seriously, Joshua, I know a couple that went for *six months* without having sex."

My jaw dropped. I tried to figure out what in the world could have gone wrong with the couple and convinced myself that it must have had to do with pregnancy. Maybe—maybe not.

Over the next few years, I had enough conversations with married men to learn that, in fact, marriage didn't guarantee good sex—it didn't guarantee sex at all. I started hearing from guys (and sometimes ladies) that I should accept the fact that even if I did have sex with my wife frequently, my wife usually wouldn't have an orgasm. It was such a disappointment to hear, so I just kept telling myself that my wife and I would be the exception.

I came to marriage with a Garden of Eden–like awe and wonder about sex, which is fairly remarkable considering the fact that I had dabbled in porn as an adult. I really believed that the climax of lovemaking would be the simple fact that, in our moments of intimacy, Raquel and I would supernaturally be one in some deeply mysterious way. I saw sex as this wonderfully bizarre and erotic sci-fi connection of bodies, a sacred privilege reserved for my marriage bed. I also thought that connection alone would bring its own pleasure and the rest would eventually fall into place. I was right.

Starting on our wedding night, I figured out a lot just by using some basic advice from a couple of guy friends, my dad, and Kevin Leman's book *Sheet Music*. Basically, affirm your wife's beauty, take your time, and have fun figuring out how to make friction work for the two of you. Also, at the advice of another friend, I brought a bunch of tea candles with me on our honeymoon to the Riviera Maya in Mexico.

At our resort, we toasted each other while reclining on canopies next to the Gulf of Mexico. There were long walks on the beach, endless supplies of exquisite appetizers, and candlelit dinners. We went on adventures flying over the jungle on zip lines, visiting the Mayan ruins, and swimming in the ocean. The balmy breeze, the rose petals, the palm trees—all of it was a mercifully restful time after the five months of wedding planning and bickering. And in that restful atmosphere, we began our journey into a playful, intense, fun learning experience of lovemaking.

I might not have been a sex therapist, and I forgot most of the stuff I read in *Sheet Music*, but I had all I needed: fearlessness, a willingness to learn, and a wife who wanted me. While that was true, it wasn't all there was to sex, which could get more complicated than I imagined, but it would take me years to learn that.

The Basics

It's amazing what a romantic, carefree resort vacation can do for your sex life. It gave us the momentum to come home and keep honeymooning for months. But then our love made three babies (whom my wife stayed at home with), my job was stressful, and we moved twice. We bought two homes, waded through the grief of drawn-out family conflicts, and struggled each day to keep the house clean. Over time, having a good sex life took serious work, and the hard work started with the most practical of things: bedtime.

Ever since we got married, Raquel and I have gone to bed at the same time. Being in our room hanging out gives us an opportunity to be around each other without the agitation of things like work, kids, and cleaning up. At the same time, it has exponentially increased the opportunities to have sex. Think about it: Our teeth are brushed, we're partially clothed, and it's not too late—why not?

A lot of the foreplay that gets things going for us happens

way before bedtime. It happens during moments when we make a concerted effort to speak each other's "love language," as Gary Chapman describes it in his long-running bestseller *The 5 Love Languages*. Chapman says that a spouse will primarily receive love through one of five categories: words of affirmation, gifts, acts of service, quality time, or physical touch (he says that a spouse usually has a secondary language as well). As Chapman explains, you've got to say "I love you" to your spouse in a way the other person understands, or your message will probably get lost in translation. I think, when it comes to sex, Chapman's paradigm is particularly helpful.

The foreplay that happens long before Raquel and I have sex is speaking each other's love language during the day. Raquel needs me to spend quality time with her; otherwise, when it comes time for sex, we'll need to spend a lot of quality time together before she's ready to go. It's not that she's withholding sex (she doesn't do that), she just needs me to be emotionally intimate with her before it feels natural for her to want to be physically intimate. On the other hand, my love language is a tie between words of affirmation and physical touch. All Raquel has to do is say, "You look hot," touch my hand, and I'm ready to go.

The point of all this early-in-the-day foreplay is that we don't just get our sexual needs met at night. We get our emotional needs met throughout the day, which only strengthens the bonds that we later reaffirm with our bodies. Frankly, however, sometimes we get lazy and don't put the time and energy into speaking in a way that fills our emotional "love tanks," as Chapman calls them.

That's exasperating and even depressing, but it is never an excuse to get our emotional or sexual needs met by anyone else. We're the exclusive source for each other.

When it comes to my emotional needs, I've made a point to keep distance from women who gravitate toward me and engage with me in an uncomfortably friendly way. For example, a few years ago, an attractive, single woman who had joined our church regularly began approaching me and striking up conversations. I was friendly at first, but then I started noticing that she would come over and talk with me in a way that had this slightly flirtatious familiarity to it. I also noticed that in volunteer meetings, she always found her way to the seat next to me and tried to start up a conversation. She knew I had a wife, but even so, she kept approaching me in a way that no other single woman was doing at our church. I told Raquel that I thought the woman was flirting with me, and I committed to avoiding the woman. After that, when she approached me to talk, I would keep the conversation short and slightly cool. I also started moving when she would come sit next to me. She withdrew, and that was that.

Some people might say that it was over the top for me to make such a big deal of what might have been an insecure woman who was just being socially awkward with a guy who's known for being unusually friendly. Do you know why I made a big deal of it? Because there's a part of me that liked the attention, and I'm afraid of that part of me. Better men than me have met a woman, slowly conceded the ground of emotional intimacy, and, in the natural doldrums of marriage, suddenly found themselves getting their emotional and sexual needs met outside of the home. I could just as easily be that guy—all it would take is a little more banter, another warm smile, and enjoying that surge of adrenaline when my arm is touched a little longer than it was last time.

Extramarital intimacy of whatever kind takes some effort. You've got to get chummy with another person without other people noticing. There's also the inconvenience of setting up rendezvous points and, of course, the part where you get caught and prove to the world that you really don't love your spouse that much.

But if you want to go whole hog with adultery and easily be more discreet about it, all you've got to do is get out your phone and find a convenient place to watch some porn. "I tell you," Jesus said, "that anyone who looks at a woman lustfully has already committed adultery with her in his heart" (Matthew 5:28). So, yeah, porn is basically adultery on the go—not just a bad habit. Porn makes a sport of visual adultery, and that's why neither Raquel nor I look at porn or watch movies with sex scenes in them. It's just as dark and demonic as sleeping with your new friend from church, but it's all the more insidious because there are no apparent consequences other than tolerating the feelings of guilt and shame after you're done partaking in it. Plus, after you get addicted to it, guilt and shame seem like a small price to pay for the high you get off cartoonishly unrealistic sex scenes that fuel a blasé attitude toward your spouse.

Pope John Paul described the emptiness of porn this way: "The problem with pornography is not that it shows too much, but that it shows too little." Porn shows bodies and sex acts, but it can't show those tender moments in the marital bed when a husband sheepishly asks, "Does that feel good?" In porn, you can't experience the eye-to-eye contact between two people who have fought hard for their marriage and have forgiven a multitude of sins. Porn can't replicate the laughter between a husband and wife who know each other's inside jokes and don't get embarrassed by the comical moments that happen sometimes during love-making. If I'm willing to forfeit all of *that* for the pitiful pleasure of being a Peeping Tom, I've surrendered my manhood. Real sex is out of reach.

Anything that meets my sexual needs other than my wife—be it porn or masturbation—is a declaration of independence from Raquel. It says, "I don't need you, honey. I can take care of myself." I don't want that. I want to starve myself of any other source of emotional and sexual gratification so that when I'm in need, Raquel is my only source.

Scripture speaks clearly about how valuable and mutually beneficial sex is for a couple. It assumes we'll have sexual needs, and it makes it clear where those needs should be met: "Each man should have his own wife, and each woman should have her own husband. The husband should fulfill his wife's sexual needs, and the wife should fulfill her husband's needs" (1 Corinthians 7:2–3 NLT). Raquel is mine and I'm hers. I meet Raquel's sexual needs and she meets mine. If we need emotional or sexual gratification, we know where to find it. It's in the sacred space of our marriage— the only place where we can experience true intimacy.

When it comes to emotional and sexual boundaries, there are plenty of walls I place around myself—friends who hold me accountable, honesty with Raquel, and vigilance with what I view on the internet—but walls can only provide so much protection. There's nothing other than my love for God and Raquel that makes any real difference in my desire to protect my marriage. That love is something we solidify together in the intimacy of worship, prayer, and the deep soul work of spiritual formation, which I talked about in chapter 4. All those things are manifested in the intimacy we experience with our bodies. That's where the truest, strongest intimacy begins; anything offered by the world, the flesh, and the devil is nothing but a cheap substitute.

Staying Connected

Something that has made a big difference in keeping our sex life strong is my willingness to initiate. Like I mentioned before, when I was single, I was aghast at the possibility that a married couple could go for months without having sex. I didn't know how a couple could get to such an awful low point.

Before Raquel and I got married, I made a promise to myself that I would do everything in my power to make sure that we had sex at least a couple of times a week. We still have that goal; however, as kids, work, and general life maintenance have crowded out the space for sex to happen more naturally, we have had to work harder for our times of physical intimacy. Some of that has to do with how different Raquel and I are.

When I get to the end of the day and I'm worn out, sex is

exactly what I want. It's the perfect stress reliever. On the other hand, when Raquel falls into bed at the end of the day and she feels like she had to fight her way to get there, sex can feel like another thing on the checklist. To get her to the place that she's willing to have sex requires some sensitivity to her emotional state. Sometimes, Raquel will tell me that she doesn't have the desire and/or the emotional bandwidth for sex. When that happens, I think it's important for me to respect that and give her some space. First Corinthians 7:3 says, "The husband should fulfill his marital duty to his wife, and likewise the wife to her husband" (NLT), but that doesn't mean the husband has the right to demand that she do so, nor should he pout until she gives in. No doubt, I feel disappointed when Raquel is not up for sex, but I don't feel dejected or rejected, and it has everything to do with the fact that I trust Raquel.

If Raquel didn't honestly mean that she's drained, she wouldn't make up excuses to get out of making love to me. I know she loves me enough to have sex when she can, and I love her enough to respect her need for space in those occasional times when it's just too much to ask of her. She's not withholding; she's just being honest. And she always reschedules when it's possible (of course, there are also alternatives to intercourse). As a friend once told me, "Nothing good will ever come from questioning your wife's reasons for not wanting to have sex." And I would add, when there's a reservoir of trust, you won't feel like you need to question them anyway.

Sometimes Raquel's not in the mood but she's still willing.

When that happens, I have to avoid the temptation to get insecure about the fact that there's a lack of enthusiasm. I've also got to be willing to slow down and give her the time and attention that it requires for both of us to enjoy ourselves. Doing those two things does not, however, guarantee that we're going to have mind-blowing sex, and that's OK. Whenever sex is kind of vanilla, I try not to focus on the lack of fireworks. That's a challenge, but every single time, I remind myself that we're still participating in this mysterious, supernatural phenomenon in which our bodies unite and we become one (1 Corinthians 6:15–16). That fact alone is so encouraging to me because it takes me back to the fundamental truth that sex is, by nature, amazing—no matter how I may feel.

One of the things that can make it so hard to have space for sex is raising kids. God knows how much we love them, but they're so needy and exasperating sometimes. They especially drain energy from Raquel, who's a stay-at-home mom. After having three children pulling at her all day, being groped by me doesn't always seem tantalizing. It takes intentionality to get the kids out of the way. So to make that happen, we put them in bed early and firmly order them not to holler for us unless there is a serious medical emergency. Sex is critical to keeping our relationship healthy, and that's our priority—it is not, however, a priority to respond to a child's request to go to the bathroom or get a drink of water.

None of these attempts to strengthen our sex life would be complete or truly effective if it weren't for the fact that Raquel and I are intentional about connecting spiritually. It's the most essential thing about who we are as a couple. We pray, read Scripture together, sit in silence before God, and ask for prayer from each other. Figuring out how to develop a consistent spiritually intimate connection has made it all the more natural to go to physically intimate places together. As they say, the couple that prays together, stays together—literally.

What Your Sex Life Reveals

I'm not trying to hold us up as the example of a couple that really knows how to do sex. I'm sharing because I want you to see that sex is a reflection of everything else in this book.

If you look back over the description of our sex life and compare it to our daily life as a couple, you'll notice something: They mirror each other.

We not only want our bodies to be as close as possible as often as possible, we want to be as emotionally close as possible, even when we're struggling with the day-to-day stresses that naturally come with marriage. That means we remain in a posture of humility with respect to each other's nonsexual needs, which still requires us to learn as we go and remember to stay attentive to each other's love languages.

We've got similar rhythms of life, and we guard against developing any exclusive emotional ties with someone of the opposite sex. That's why, outside of exceptional situations, I don't spend time alone with another woman and Raquel doesn't spend time alone with another man. We realize that an emotional connection can be just as tempting as a physical one. We have deep friendships with people of the same sex, but even then, when it comes to our most intimate emotional needs, we are the exclusive source of meeting those needs for each other.

I deeply engage with Raquel by starting conversations with her and praying for her. Connection in conversation is part of the lifeblood of our relationship. Something would be wrong with us if we weren't praying together at least a little bit every day. Conversation and prayer sound easy, but—just like with sex—it takes work to make those spiritual connections happen, especially because kids demand so much attention.

Sometimes one of us is more eager to connect in prayer (usually Raquel) or conversation (usually me). She might need to be a little patient, and I might need to be open to trying, even if it's just a little prayer time and reading a chapter of the Bible together. If I just give it a little effort, before we know it, we're having a deeply meaningful prayer time or conversation.

Look at what you and your spouse are like as a couple day to day, and compare it to what your sex life is like. You'll find that there's a great deal of overlap. If you're playful with each other when you're hanging out in the yard, you'll be playful in between the sheets. If you have meaningful conversations when you're alone in the living room, your physical connection in the bedroom will be more meaningful as well. If you make the effort to stay emotionally connected when people and problems threaten to pull you apart, you'll fight off the temptations that tempt you to find sexual fulfillment elsewhere.

The purpose of this chapter isn't to make you feel condemned because your sex life isn't that great at the moment. It's to encourage you to do everything you can to make physical intimacy happen in your marriage, whatever the cost—even when the desire for it isn't always reciprocated. If that sounds like an insurmountable task, that's because it *is* an insurmountable task that can only happen if your heart is overflowing with the unconditional love of Jesus.

Unconditional love says, "I may feel totally disconnected from you emotionally, but I'm going to keep making conversation with you, affirming you, serving you, surprising you with gifts, and/ or spontaneously reaching over to touch your hand." That kind of love says, "I'm going to do what I can to be sexually attractive to you and arouse you. I'll humbly take no for an answer. I'll have sex with you sometimes when I'm tired and don't feel like having sex. And, so help me God, I won't go to anybody but you to get the emotional and physical intimacy that I desperately need."

Viagra Humiliation at the Pharmacy

On our honeymoon, we were in a pharmacy in Mexico where there was a couple in line (in front of us) who looked to be in their fifties. The husband had short, gray hair and was a little overweight; he was wearing a T-shirt and blue jean shorts. He walked up to the counter and quietly said, "Do you sell any Viagra?"

In a voice loud enough for everyone to hear, the man behind the counter replied, "Viagra is thirty dollars a pill."

The man looked over at his wife, who looked back at him with an expression of helpless resignation. It was as if they were doing the cost/benefit analysis in their minds. On the one hand, they wanted to fool around in paradise like the old days; on the other hand, the pill was so expensive and might have even been a rip-off from the unscrupulous owner of the pharmacy.

"No thanks," said the husband faintly, and the couple quietly walked away.

I felt compassion for the couple, especially the man. I wondered if maybe he had been on a honeymoon a long time ago during which sex had been easy for him. Was it age that slowed things down? Prostate cancer? It was a horrifying thought to me—the man didn't even have a shot at pleasing his wife without a pill that he couldn't afford.

"God, I pray that never happens to me," I said to myself, never dreaming it actually would.

Barbarians at the Gate

In the fall of our ninth year of marriage, I was under severe stress due to an overwhelming workload at the office, an excruciating treatment I was undergoing for a chronic illness, and the emotional weight of coping with the news that my dad had only weeks left to live. I also felt like I was failing as a husband and father because I didn't have the time to be available to my wife and kids. The anxiety was beginning to show at home.

Sometimes I would break down in front of my family after saying goodbye to Dad on the phone. He had always been so sharp and animated, but almost overnight, his thoughts were becoming muddled and difficult to follow. It was crushing me that there was nothing I could do to save him. I was also getting home later and later, and when I walked in the door, I would be greeted by a listless hello from Raquel, who had been with children for twelve hours straight. I would apologize and then bound up the stairs to see the kids, but the lights would already be off.

"Daddy," Layla said in the dark one night when I got home at eight thirty, "can you please get home earlier so you can play with us?"

"Yeah," I said, feeling a wave of guilt, "I'll do everything I can to get home by seven o'clock tomorrow."

"I miss you, Daddy."

"I know. I miss you too."

The crushing weight of all the instability began hijacking my soundness of mind, but the fog had come so gradually that I confused depression with "just going through a really hard time." Even so, there was one place left untouched by the battle raging around and inside of me: our bedroom, my refuge.

One night, during a moment of intimacy, something went wrong. It was like my body just gave up for no reason. It had never happened before.

"I don't know what just happened," I said, clearly shaken. "I'm sorry."

"You don't need to apologize," Raquel said.

"I know, but—that's never happened."

"It's fine, Joshua."

It *wasn't* fine, though. I was mortified—the gates of the Garden of Eden had been breached. For nine years, I'd felt like a champ in bed, privately proud that I had never struggled with sexual dysfunction. Now my record was tainted. I told myself it was no big deal and it wouldn't happen again. But the next time, to my horror, it did.

And the next time.

And the time after that.

And the time after that.

It got to the point that when I knew we were going to have sex, I would feel this internal earthquake that would start rocking the very center of my core. I would have to force myself to breathe at a normal pace to keep my body from shaking. My sex drive had been taken hostage, and I was terrified that I would never get it back.

I finally went to the urologist and asked what was wrong with me. He asked a series of questions and did an examination, and then he issued the verdict.

"Listen man," said the young doctor, "there's nothing wrong with your equipment. You're just scared for some reason, and your fight-or-flight reaction is kicking in. When that happens, it feels like you're about to fight a bear. Your body can't keep things going if your brain is telling you that you're going to die."

I didn't know what I was afraid of. After nine years of great sex, I had no reason to believe sex was some kind of threat. Plus, even though the breakdowns had repeatedly happened, Raquel had done nothing but assure me that God was at work in the circumstances and that she was still attracted to me. None of this helped me feel any better or any less afraid it would happen again.

"I'm so sorry," I said to Raquel after another crash and burn. "Something's wrong with me. I really am sorry."

"Cut it out, Joshua," Raquel said casually. "You have nothing to be sorry for. I'm totally OK."

"Well, *I'm* not," I said. "I really am sorry. I do appreciate you trying to make me feel better when this happens, but I know you're disappointed."

"Let me assure you," she said, "I'm a happy woman, and this doesn't change that at all. We'll just keep trying."

"Well, that's nice of you to say," I said half-heartedly as I walked into the closet to get dressed.

"You'd better be careful about what you're saying to yourself right now. This doesn't define you," Raquel called out.

But I had no control of what I was saying to myself. I was overwhelmed with defeat and all my dejected thoughts were running together: "I'm a failure. Something is permanently wrong with me. She will never enjoy sex again. I'm going to be like that guy at the pharmacy. My life as I've known it is over. I will never be able to apologize enough for the way I've failed Raquel. I'm so *stupid.*"

I stepped out of the closet and looked at Raquel.

"Seriously, I'm sorry."

"Stop it," Raquel replied firmly. "You have to be careful, Joshua. You've got too much of your identity tied up in this. God is taking you on a journey, and it's more important than how things go during sex."

I stared at her with my jaw clenched.

"I just want to go back to the way things were before."

"No, you don't. God's taking you somewhere better. You've been performing in a lot of ways over the years, including in the bedroom, and it's not working anymore. God's calling you to something higher than a performance, and you're going to work through this with Him, however long that takes. I don't mind waiting on that."

The Unwanted Journey

One night, after another breakdown, I was lying in bed in the dark with my jaw clenched, my hands in white-knuckled fists, and tears running down my face. Anytime we were having sex and I had the fearful thought that I would fail again, you could count on it: It was over.

"Joshua," Raquel said, "this doesn't define you."

I didn't respond. I didn't care what she said about my identity. I just wanted to be good at sex again.

"Joshua?" she said.

"Yeah?" I replied, wiping away tears, grateful that it was dark and Raquel couldn't see me.

"I'm not going anywhere," she said.

The words hit me in the chest and took me back to that day at the Tomb of the Unknown Soldier in Arlington National Cemetery when I admitted my sexual brokenness to her. Back then, I felt sure she would leave me once she knew what a mess I was. But here she was, saying it again. And when the words sunk in, something hit me: I really was afraid she was going to leave me.

I couldn't believe such a thought would've ever entered my mind. Perhaps, I wondered, it had always been there. Maybe it had to do with the fact that my dad left my mom five times. Maybe I thought my ability to please my wife sexually was the thing that made me a valuable husband (or a man). It didn't really matter. What was for sure was that my weakness didn't define me as a husband. The revelation reminded me of this passage: "Concerning this thing I pleaded with the Lord three times that it might depart from me. And He said to me, 'My grace is sufficient for you, for My strength is made perfect in weakness'" (2 Corinthians 12:8–9 NKJV).

It would be nice to say that, at that point, I had an emotional and spiritual breakthrough and my sex life instantly turned around, but that wasn't the case. In the following weeks, having pleasurable sex was hit or miss, depending on how stressed out I was. I still berated myself internally, but it helped to remind myself that my sex life was really just a reflection of where we were as a couple. I was the weak one, the one having constant breakdowns in the face of extreme stress and exhausting depression. My confidence was shot, and I felt impotent in almost every area of my life. Of course I was going to struggle in the bedroom. I was barely grateful for this thorn in my side—at least it drew me to Jesus. I didn't really have a choice but to be grateful. I either had to reframe my nightmare or crumble into an even darker despair.

"If you can just slowly climb back to a more stable place without all these confidence-crushing stressors," I told myself, "things will eventually get better." I found that to be true, though the journey back was arduous, especially because some of the unbearable stresses ended up being replaced by others. I survived, and though it has taken a long time to recover, I know I couldn't have done it without Jesus. I also know that Raquel was the manifestation of His grace during one of the darkest, most emasculating times of my life.

Raquel put my needs above hers when she chose to be gracious to me *every single* time I came apart. Not *once* did she criticize me or act exasperated with my inability to "perform." And it should come as no surprise that, since then, outside the bedroom, we have slowly become more tender with each other than ever before. My grief became a source of grace.

Finding God in the Messiness

There's something Mike Mason wrote in *The Mystery of Marriage* that meant very little to me when I read it years ago, but it speaks volumes to me now:

> What the sex life really demands is the loving gift of the self, the sincere devotion of the whole heart. Where this is present, problems such as impotence, premature ejaculation, or inability to achieve orgasm will fade into insignificance and in time may well disappear. Only love can really cope with (let alone heal) such things.

If you and/or your spouse are experiencing sexual dysfunction, don't give up on romance; don't give up on sexually connecting, no matter how abysmal the results seem to be. In those
tender, heart-wrenching moments, you can fall into each other's
arms and know that, orgasms or not, you're never going to give
up on each other. There in the grief you've discovered in your
marriage bed, you can experience intimacy like you never have
before. In lovemaking, you come home to the Garden of Eden;
in that place, you get to experience what it feels like to be naked
and unashamed (Genesis 2:25; 3:10). It's the place we're all search-
ing for in one way or another. In that gracious manifestation of
the love of Christ, Satan's accusations fall on deaf ears. There's no
reason to hide anymore.

7

For Better
or Worse

ONE AFTERNOON DURING MY SECOND YEAR OF MARRIAGE, I HAD
a troubling experience. I was at a party talking to someone when
all of a sudden, I felt like I was in a dream. I struggled to remember how to say basic words for about thirty seconds; then suddenly, everything went back to normal. I went over to a friend and
described what had just happened.

"Maybe you have superpowers," he replied with a chuckle.

I was spooked, but I shook it off until the next day when I was
at work typing and it suddenly happened again. I looked down at
the keyboard and couldn't make sense of the letters as I tried to

continue typing; when I came out of it, I looked at the screen and realized that the words were nothing more than a mishmash of incoherent letters.

The thirty-second episodes kept happening with greater intensity, causing me to wonder if I had brain cancer or something else. So I went to a neurologist, who thought I might be having painless migraines. He ordered brain scans, which didn't reveal anything. That became all the more disturbing as the episodes picked up more momentum and brought on new symptoms, all of which affected language. Over and over again, I had these thirty-second intervals where I couldn't read, write, or type, and I had trouble speaking.

Finally I visited the Mayo Clinic in Florida, and after a week-long battery of tests, a specialist came into the room and bluntly delivered the diagnosis: "Mr. Rogers, you have epilepsy." Then he explained the reason for the language interference: My particular form of epilepsy is limited to the part of my brain that processes language. Raquel was unfazed by it and encouraged me to believe that God was going to heal me, but I wasn't confident about that. Raquel and I had been praying for me to be healed since the episodes had started, and God still hadn't stopped them. Now I had the news that they weren't just "episodes"; they were seizures.

I hated the diagnosis. It made me feel so strange and gross. Epilepsy had a negative connotation to it, kind of like "mental illness." The people with epilepsy in the movies and TV shows always fell on the ground and flopped around, foaming at the mouth. And, of course, there was the word some people would use to describe me: *epileptic.* I hated that word and would correct people.

"I'm not an 'epileptic.' I am someone *who has* epilepsy. You wouldn't call someone with cancer a cancer-eptic."

Even though my doctor had cleared me to drive, if people knew I had epilepsy, they frequently asked the question I hated: "Are you *sure* you're safe to drive?" Even worse was when people would be talking to me—sometimes in public—and bluntly ask, "How are you doing with epilepsy?" I got so tired of it that one time when a guy from church came up and asked the question, I replied, "It's fine. How's your rectal health?"

The most embarrassing moments were when I lost my words in the middle of conversations. To hide it from whomever I was talking to, I would put my fingers to my temple and silently wait for the attack to pass. When I would come out of it and people would ask if I was OK, I would just tell them that I'd had a "little migraine thing." This obviously didn't work with Raquel, who saw it regularly, and I hated that.

"It's happening, isn't it?" she would ask when I suddenly lost my words.

I would just nod and—when I came out of it—feel embarrassed, even though it didn't bother Raquel. It bothered me, though. It was a crack in my armor—kryptonite. There was a part of me that was still trying to impress Raquel. Impressive to me, as a husband, meant that I was strong.

Vulnerability Is Humiliating

For the first few years of our marriage, I was quick to support Raquel and help her deal with what she was going through, but she often had no idea when I was struggling and needed help. I would've never acknowledged it at the time, but the imbalance of vulnerability created an emotional imbalance in our marriage. It didn't bother me. I was the one who was OK—at least I usually appeared to be—and I liked it that way. She was the needy one. I had it together.

I'm willing to bet that in your marriage one of you is the more vulnerable, needy one. It could be a function of personality, but either way, if there's one of you who somehow happens to be OK all the time (like I was), something's off-kilter. I didn't want to talk to Raquel about my weaknesses and insecurities. I preferred to talk to my guy friends (thank God I had them). I was too proud to show my pain. I was the man of the house. I was "Tigger," as she called me.

When I talk about being vulnerable with your spouse, I'm talking about all the stuff we hide from each other: the monumental stuff like sexual brokenness I described in the previous chapter (for the record, I put it in its own chapter because sexual vulnerability is in a league of its own). Then there are health problems (physical and mental), child-raising struggles, and work issues, to name a few. There are also the nitty-gritty sinful impulses in your heart, like the way you nurse petty wounds, think you're better than your least favorite sinner, or feel insecure about not getting enough positive feedback on social media—the kind of stuff you don't even admit to yourself.

If it sounds terrifying to you to open up and reveal that kind of stuff to your spouse, ask yourself why. What do you have to hide? What do you have to lose in telling the truth to your spouse? What are all the things your spouse doesn't know? Are you sharing this stuff with *anybody*?

I'm sure you want intimacy with your spouse. Awkward, invasive vulnerability is your chance to take it to the next level. If you're anything like me, however, it will take outside pressure to force out the real you.

Scrambled Emotions

In the years that followed my early days of epilepsy, the episodes remained steady; while the obvious solution would've been to increase the dosage of my medication, I was hoping to manage my disorder naturally somehow. I had changed medications four times in the first seven years since being diagnosed, and the side effects of the drugs were disruptive, to one degree or another. One drug made me forgetful and dull; one quit working after three months; and another made me act like an irritable, drunk guy (just ask the man on the bus with a tattoo of a bar code on his neck who encouraged me to get an identical one—I told him I wouldn't do such a thing because, and I quote, "I'm not a loser").

As I continued to privately wrestle with having my brain regularly ambushed by these episodes that literally left me at a loss for words, I became despondent about my chances of ever being healed. I had prayed for healing hundreds upon hundreds of times, often with Raquel, and she began to hear the exasperation in my voice, the panic.

"God," I would plead with Raquel by my side, "please heal me. You can heal anyone. What are You waiting for? If my child were sick and I had the medication to heal her, nothing would stop me. Please make it stop, God."

The more I prayed, the more I felt like God was indifferent to my plea for healing, until my ninth year of marriage when I stumbled upon a treatment that gave me hope.

I had written an article about finding God on the journey of having epilepsy, and an old friend responded by sending me a message about the Ketogenic Diet Center at Johns Hopkins Hospital. The hospital has had relatively high success rates in treating patients with epilepsy using an extremely high-fat, low-carbohydrate diet. The basic science behind how the diet works is that without carbohydrates giving you energy, your body produces ketones as a substitute. Somehow, those ketones help stabilize the neurons in the brain—my dream come true.

I eagerly signed up for the astringent diet, assuming my pathological self-discipline would help me power through. I had no idea what I was getting into. Unlike the recreational ketogenic fad diet, in which there's a degree of flexibility, treatment of epilepsy with the diet is an intense regimen requiring that you eat approximately twenty grams of carbohydrates per day. There are no cheat days.

When I got in my car to drive to Johns Hopkins for the diet orientation, I discovered a note that my five-year-old daughter, Layla, had left me: "I hop you haVe a grate day dad. I wilL prae for you." I figured with the prayers of my wife and daughters, combined with the world-class treatment at Johns Hopkins, epilepsy didn't stand a chance.

Within two days of starting the extremely low-carb diet, I felt disoriented and experienced flu-like symptoms. I didn't care. I figured my body was just working the keto magic, rewiring my brain and creating new, healthy connections that would suppress the irregular brain impulses that had been scrambling letters and words in my head for years. With that optimism firmly in place, I underplayed the negative effects when Raquel asked how things were going during that first week. I had a lot of work to do at the office, which I could hardly concentrate on, but I didn't want her thinking that I was too weak to do my job. So, I told her that I was doing well overall, but that I could feel my body "adjusting." In that conversation and many others in the coming days, I just kept covering up the physical and emotional symptoms that plagued me. I was having enough trouble keeping the diet going, and I didn't need her to stress me out any more with her worrying.

Around the time I began the diet, we learned that our one-year-old son was severely lactose intolerant. This meant that if Raquel was going to cook, she had to make three meals (one for our son, one for her and our daughters, and one for me). She couldn't do that, and I didn't have the time or the motivation to spend hours making the keto-friendly meals I found online. Plus, half of them were disgusting concoctions of low-carb ingredients drenched in coconut oil and/or butter. So, I just started making the same eight meals every week, measuring every serving of spinach down to the leaf and drinking about a cup of oil every day (it was a quick way to get the proper level of fat intake). I felt repulsed almost every time I ate.

The first time my frustration broke through the dam of prideful deception happened one morning when I accidentally ate too many blackberries at breakfast and realized I had blown through seven of my twenty allotted carbs for the day. I was standing in the kitchen when I realized it, and in a burst of anger, I spontaneously smacked the blackberries against the backsplash, knocking the plastic container open and causing them to roll onto the counter. Raquel and the girls saw it happen and stood there looking at me in silence. I looked down, startled by my own behavior, and said, with a quiet tone of angry sadness, "I hate this diet."

In the weeks that followed, I became fixated on having just one day without a single episode. I was so obsessed that this goal became my daily measure of my success or failure in life. I thought about it all day. It was the main subject of conversation with Raquel and my friends. I weighed every ounce of food I ate. I started consuming 325 grams of fat per day and just 10 grams of carbohydrates, which Johns Hopkins had never recommended. To my great disappointment, however, the diet didn't cure me of epilepsy, but the number of episodes did plunge by about

75 percent after a couple of months, which my doctor considered a success. The encouraging signs only stoked my neurotic determination as I kept telling myself that, one day, if I just tried a little harder, I was finally going to have my breakthrough.

Day by day, I failed to meet my goal. I started giving in to hopelessness until eventually, my normally sunny and enthusiastic disposition all but faded. There was no more faking it with Raquel. I couldn't get away from the diet, which followed me everywhere. Every cereal box at the grocery store, every slice of bread, every high-carb piece of watermelon was a reminder that I was a food freak. It was on my mind all day long. All I wanted was to be healed.

Spiritual Vulnerability

I started living with this low-grade sense of panic over the diet, and my anxiety began to spill over into other areas of my life. At work, I became perpetually anxious. And as I mentioned in the previous chapter, the fear even found its way into my bedroom and crashed my sex life, which was utterly devastating. My life was becoming a nightmare, but I had come too far to turn around. I was a gambler at the slot machine. The escalation of commitment had locked me in, and I wasn't going to stop putting quarters in the machine until I hit the jackpot.

In the midst of the breakdown, the doctors told my brother and me that my dad had only weeks or months to live. I couldn't handle it. I had worked so hard to help him get on track with his health; all my efforts seemed to be for nothing. In a useless attempt to rescue him, I called him almost every day to make sure he was cooperating with his doctors. He was having trouble communicating as his brain got less and less oxygen and his thoughts became disjointed. I would get off the phone after talking with him on my morning commute and start brushing the tears away. I knew I was losing him, and I was grieving in advance of the inevitable.

Whatever modicum of emotional restraint I'd had with Raquel flew out the window in the midst of the crisis that just kept metastasizing. During times of prayer with Raquel, I started furiously begging God to finish the healing. Then it came Raquel's turn to pray, and she would utter these earnest prayers, asking God to help me be aware of His presence in the journey. I bristled a few times when she prayed that way.

"Do you really have to pray that?" I would ask. "It feels like a guilt trip. Like you think I haven't reached some magical point where I've learned all I needed to learn from this nightmare. I just want to be healed."

"He is going to heal you, Joshua," she would say. "But I think He wants to heal your heart, not just your brain, and He's using this diet to get down into some deep places inside that you're not even aware of."

"Well, I hope He gets there soon."

I didn't want Raquel to be right. Her words sounded similar to passages like James 1:2–4: "Consider it pure joy, my brothers and sisters, whenever you face trials of many kinds, because you know that the testing of your faith produces perseverance. Let perseverance finish its work so that you may be mature and complete, not lacking anything."

I didn't want perseverance to "finish its work." It felt like it was going to finish me off. I wanted this season to be over; I wanted to be one of the success stories at Johns Hopkins, to get in front of everybody at church and testify that I had experienced a miracle.

Day after day, I counted the seizures one by one, feeling like a failure every time I had one. But in the midst of this storm, I found surprising consolation in confessing my weakness and fear to Raquel. Vulnerability had become a source of comfort. The tables had completely turned, and I didn't care anymore.

I'd been the one who always had the faith, the one who was always finding God in the ordinary. I'd been the one with advice, the one with words of wisdom for other people. That was over. All I could do was confess my unbelief, trust that I was on a journey with Jesus, and hold out hope that Raquel was right about me getting healed.

Raquel wasn't the only one who was helping me hold on to hope. My daughters played a significant role in keeping me encouraged as well. They regularly laid hands on my head and prayed for me, and sometimes they made the most confident proclamations of faith that I was going to be healed. On one of those occasions, we all went to Walmart for everyone (but me) to pick out a pint of ice cream for the "family ice cream taste test."

When we returned, my seven-year-old daughter, Giselle, asked with enthusiasm, "Dad, are you excited about the *family ice cream taste test*?"

Her question stung. One of the hardest things about the keto diet was the exclusion from enjoying food with other people, but being excluded from a moment like that with my *family*—it hurt far more than not being able to eat a piece of cake in the break room at work.

"I can't have that ice cream," I said. "You're not supposed to eat it when you're on this diet."

Giselle looked up, her eyes watered, and she wrapped her arms around my legs.

"I'm sorry you can't eat ice cream, Daddy."

"It's OK. I need to do this so I can get to feeling better."

A few minutes after the family ice cream taste test was over, I was in the hallway when Giselle ran up to me with a big smile on her face.

"Daddy, God told me He's going to heal you."

"That's great," I said, not believing her but wishing it were true.

"You're going to be healed, Daddy!" she repeated with even more enthusiasm. I just looked at her with a mix of pity and skepticism.

"Is that what you *think* He wants to do?" I asked.

"No," she said, "that's what He *told* me He's going to do."

I couldn't help but believe her. God's healing was my only hope.

"You really believe He's going to take away these seizures?"

She looked at me with joyful confidence.

"He sure is. It's all on the cross, Dad."

Places You've Never Been

As humiliating as it sometimes felt to be such a needy, broken mess as a husband, it took my spiritual intimacy with Raquel far beyond anywhere it had been before. We were both undone a lot of the time, but at least we were undone together, and it was pushing both of us to lean hard on the Lord. Like our broken sex life, which was more intimate than ever in its own way, our spiritual life was going to deep places that we had never known before. Our connection couldn't help but become more intimate. We were laid bare and desperate for His deliverance, and we found new comfort in psalms of lament like Psalm 69: "Save me, O God! For the waters have come up to my neck. I sink in deep mire . . . I am weary with my crying; my throat is dry; my eyes fail while I wait for my God" (verses 1–3 NKJV).

When I think back on this crushing time of stress on our marriage, I feel like telling spouses—men in particular—not to put off lowering your guard with your spouse. If there's any reason for you and your spouse to practice vulnerability, which is really just a form of honesty, it's to find the freedom of being real with each other and God. There's nothing to hide. The lower you're willing to go together into the depths of spiritual despair, the more earnestly you'll be able to celebrate those highs of God's deliverance together—as Raquel and I eventually did.

Whatever distress you may be experiencing, start seeking the

Lord together. If you don't know what to pray, sit in the same room together, open your hands before Him, and ask Him to fill both of you. Pick a psalm of lament or praise, read through it together, and then use it as the language of your prayer. Lift up specific praises to God, going back and forth as your spirits are lifted high together. In those times, you will discover—as you hold on to each other—that the "joy of the LORD is your strength" (Nehemiah 8:10 ESV), which is the only strength you've got in those dark hours.

Open Invitation

In the midst of the diet, one of my greatest concerns with my emotional state was that I didn't want Raquel to have to dig through the rubble every day and pull me out. That's where my closest friends came through for me and, indirectly, for her. One friend in particular, Shon, helped hold me together as I kept falling apart. Vulnerability was key.

I called Shon at least twice a week for months as the crisis went on, and I told him about everything: my fears that Dad would end up in a nursing facility; the fear that I was just one court deadline away from a major mistake at work; and I even shared the humiliating details of my broken sex life. I was so desperate for a listening ear that I didn't even care.

God knows the number of times I called Shon and tried to make sense of what was happening. I would call him on the way home from the gym early in the morning and start talking . . . and keep talking and talking. I would go for ten minutes straight without stopping and Shon would just listen—really listen. Long after I had parked the car in the driveway and I was still going, he would stay present with me, taking it in, listening. It wasn't the kind of listening where someone bears with you until you talk yourself into a solution. It felt more like the Holy Spirit had taken over Shon's ears, and my grief was going from his eardrums to Jesus.

There was nobody other than Raquel who knew as much of my grief and the fear that was taking over. I don't know how she and I would've made it without Shon. If anything, she would've been bearing more of the stress of my constant breakdowns, and I don't know if that was possible. To this day, she will tell you what Shon's constant availability meant to her: In walking through the crisis with me, he was walking through it with her too.

Avocado Oil and Taco Breakdown

A wedding reception was the beginning of the end of the keto diet.

On a breezy fall day, Raquel and I drove through the rural foothills of Maryland to attend the wedding of a dear friend. I should've been happy—we had prayed for the right mate for our friend for many years—but I felt listless and emotionally dry.

I stared forward as I drove, making dull conversation with Raquel.

"Are you OK?" she asked.

"Of course not, Raquel," I snapped. "It's just going to be another event where I have to avoid all of the good food and pretend like I'm having a good time."

She didn't argue with me. She knew I was right.

The ceremony itself was moving as the couple said their vows with the sun setting behind them, but it was all downhill for me after the groom kissed the bride and the preacher directed everyone to walk over to the lavish reception where the feast awaited.

Servers emerged from the kitchen with tantalizing hors d'oeuvres on silver platters. My mouth watered behind a tight-lipped "No, thank you" each time a smiling server tempted me with another delectable morsel. I looked around at the other guests popping mini crab cakes into their mouths like they were going out of style and felt myself drowning in a whirlpool of jealousy, grief, and covetousness. The other guests could eat twenty of those things if they wanted, but if I ate just one, it would blow through 25 percent of my carbohydrate budget for the day.

I had eaten my disgusting keto-friendly dinner before we arrived—a crustless "pizza" made with a tablespoon of butter, two tablespoons of olive oil, spinach, cherry tomatoes, mushrooms, cheese, cheese, cheese, and more cheese. It was the same "pizza" I had made four other times that week.

In the midst of the bustling reception, the champagne, wine, and soft drinks flowed, but I passed on those and sipped on seltzer water instead. Finally, I headed for the door.

"Where are you going?" Raquel asked.

"Out to the car. I need to drink some avocado oil."

(File this under things Raquel never thought she'd hear her husband say.)

I took the seltzer water with me and used it to help me put

down the four-tablespoon shot of avocado oil before returning to the party, where guests were now filling up on the sprawling dinner buffet.

I went through the buffet line and, using my carb counter app, realized that I could only eat ten asparagus spears. I simmered with low-grade anger. I didn't want the food to go to waste, so I filled my plate, went over to my friend Randy, and dumped everything but the asparagus on his plate. Raquel leaned over to me.

"Are you going to be all right?" she asked.

"I'm fine," I said.

"No, you're not."

I stood up, got another club soda, and downed it, trying to swallow the lump in my throat. I hated the diet—the constant exclusion, being the keto guy at the party, seeing delicious food as an enemy.

The next day, my standoff with food reached its climax. We had a big taco lunch at church to celebrate our church's anniversary, but it wasn't safe for me to eat the tacos—not even the meat and cheese. I didn't know what ingredients were in the meat seasoning (God forbid, sugar); besides, I didn't have my trusty scale with me to make sure I didn't exceed my carb count. It broke my heart. The tacos were just your average high school lunchroom tacos—the ones I love, actually—so rather than get anywhere near the line, I stood on the far side of the room and played with my son, feeling depressed as I watched everyone else down their food.

When I got home from church and realized there wasn't much in the fridge, I knew we needed to go to the grocery store. But it didn't matter; pretty much everything I ate came out of the meat drawer anyway. I opened it to find five of the same ingredients I had been eating for weeks and weeks: mozzarella cheese, ham, spinach, eggs, and bacon.

I stood in front of the fridge with the doors open, staring forward. Tears filled my eyes and then ran down my cheeks. I slammed the refrigerator door, dragged myself upstairs to our bedroom, and sat on the bed for twenty minutes wiping away the tears that just kept coming. When I heard Raquel get home and start walking up the stairs to our room, I felt both relieved and embarrassed. She had seen me cry, but not like that. That kind of vulnerability was still outside of my comfort zone.

"What's going on?" she asked, stepping through the door.

There were no words. I just shook my head and wiped away tears, which were replaced with more tears. Raquel came over, sat next to me, and put her arm around me.

"I can't do it," were the only words I could squeeze past the lump in my throat. I got up and walked into the bathroom to get some toilet paper and blew my nose.

"I can't do it," I said, again and again, and slid down to the floor.

A fresh round of tears came as Raquel put her hand on my shoulder. For fifteen minutes the only thing she did was either sit in silence or whisper the name of Jesus until, finally, she spoke to me.

"I'm so sorry you're going through this," she said. "God's doing a work in you, Joshua. You're going to get through this."

"I can't," I said again.

Raquel paused.

"The Lord is with you in this, Joshua."

Known Behind the Fake Tan

A week after my bathroom breakdown, I went on a network morning show to talk about an op-ed I'd written that included a heartwarming moment from our marriage. The morning of the interview, I said goodbye to Raquel after she prayed with me, and then I drove to the studio, rehearsing again and again what I would say on camera. It's not often that a freelance writer gets to be on national TV, and I was determined to nail it, no matter how depressed I felt.

As I sat in the studio under the lights waiting to go on the air, I looked at myself in the monitor and realized that the makeup they'd put on me worked. For the first time in my life, I looked like I had a natural tan. I flashed a smile into the camera and took a deep breath to make sure I looked as relaxed as possible.

As the commercial break wound up, I heard the host in my ear giving me a heads-up about the questions he and his cohost would ask. I got ready for my response to the first question, took a deep breath, swallowed, sat up straight, and looked into the camera.

"A man's story of family, love, and faith is really resonating with our viewers," the host said, and then something interesting happened: The first thing his cohost said to me was, "Everyone wants their marriage to be perfect, but it never is," and then she followed that up by asking me to explain how growing through our struggles as a couple had impacted our kids. In response, I talked honestly about how Raquel and I had vigorously struggled for control over the years, but I assured the host that things had improved as we had both determined that we were going to grow.

The whole conversation ended up being rather surreal. There I was, suspending my depression for five minutes to talk about how Raquel and I had released control so that we could grow as a couple. Five miles away, Raquel was watching, knowing just how much control I had released by dropping my guard completely with her. Behind the smile and the fake tan, she knew me—the real me.

Finding God in the Messiness

Three months after my breakdown, I sat down with my doctor and told her I couldn't do the diet anymore. When I explained the impact it was having on me emotionally, she was taken aback. I had indicated in emails to the clinic that I felt exasperated with the diet, but plenty of patients feel that way. My doctor had had no idea that I'd crashed into full-blown depression; nor had she realized the extremes I had taken with the diet in trying to heal myself.

As I gradually stepped away from the rigors of the diet, my doctor and I focused on increasing my medication. Eventually, my seizure activity became so light that I hardly noticed it anymore (it's even less these days). While this was, in many ways, the realization of a dream of mine, there was no euphoria. There was just quiet gratitude that my brain felt 96 percent normal.

More than anything, I felt grateful for Raquel, though *grateful* really isn't the right word. I felt indebted to her, overwhelmed by her love, dumbfounded that she didn't seem to grasp how heroic her efforts were. This was a woman who had promised to walk beside me as long as we both lived—she never anticipated that she would have to throw me over her shoulders and carry me. Yet she did so without complaint and never hinted that she was doing it out of obligation. She was just loving me for who I was, even though that person wasn't the man I had ever wanted to be. When Job's life fell apart, his wife said, "Curse God and die!" (Job 2:9). When my life fell apart, my wife said, "The Lord is with you in this, Joshua."

In the words of King Lemuel: "A wife of noble character who can find? She is worth far more than rubies. Her husband has full confidence in her and lacks nothing of value" (Proverbs 31:10–11).

With Raquel, I discovered that people were right: I'd had no idea who she really was until we got married. I'd had no idea that she would love so relentlessly, that she would be such a faithful companion in the worst of times when I felt so poor in spirit. And keep in mind that it was only through the awful experience of absolute helplessness that God brought me to a place where I was finally willing to be vulnerable and throw off my facade of always being "OK."

Vulnerability in marriage is a flesh-and-blood manifestation of our relationship with Christ, the husband to the church and all believers. Nobody gets closer to us than Him. Nobody is more aware of our weaknesses and frailties. Yet we sometimes resist laying our souls bare before Him. Maybe we're afraid of what He will do when He sees us for who we are; then again, we only have to look upon the cross to address that concern.

When we are pushed past the edge of our defenses, we can be grateful for the humiliating tears our spouses see us cry, the struggles they share with us. It's practice for the way we interact with Christ. Those reluctant admissions of brokenness are rehearsals for vulnerability in prayer. The mere act of submitting our real selves in our marriage relationships can make the entire act less intimidating and make us more likely to do the same with Jesus.

Consider taking the risk of loving your spouse by being vulnerable—being your real self, emotionally naked. That's what marriage is for. It is widely believed that Augustine of Hippo, when asked what love looks like, replied, "It has the hands to help others. It has the feet to hasten to the poor and needy. It has eyes to see misery and want. It has the ears to hear the sighs and sorrows of men. That is what love looks like." Are you willing to be the kind of spouse who loves like that—one who admits how much you need that kind of love? You can't be loved "for better or worse" if your spouse doesn't know what your "better or worse" is. Give your spouse the chance to love you as you are, to love you as Jesus loves you.

8

Fully Submitted

I COULDN'T VERY WELL WRITE A BOOK ABOUT MARRIAGE without addressing the topic of submission. *Submission* and *headship* are loaded terms that can make people bristle or simply scratch their heads. But when you take a closer look at these concepts as presented in Scripture, you find that they're actually loaded with wild and wonderful, audaciously beautiful principles that can make a marriage thrive. Sadly, it took writing this book for me to really begin to get it.

Initially, I didn't think I had anything to add to the well-worn topic of submission, which felt so heavy and theological. Lord knows, I'm not a theologian. Not to mention that many others, including Tim Keller in his book *The Meaning of Marriage*, have written eloquently on the practice of submission within the marriage relationship. I couldn't totally avoid the topic, though. I was writing a book about finding God in the messiness of marriage. I couldn't just skip over the part of Scripture that gives a blueprint for how marriage is supposed to function.

Sheldon Vanauken's classic *A Severe Mercy* details the early years of his romance with his wife, Davy. One of the many ways they guarded their relationship from erosion was through the "principle of courtesy." Basically, if Sheldon asked Davy to do something inconvenient, Davy would do it graciously because she trusted that Sheldon loved her and would only inconvenience her if he had a good reason. It was a type of mutual submission, if you will.

I've never forgotten Vanauken's "principle of courtesy," and it has countless times inspired me to go downstairs and get water at Raquel's request even though I've just snuggled down under the comforter and laid my head on the pillow (a few times I've even squeezed lemon juice into the water). In those moments, I've felt as if I'm growing as a husband, one cup of cold water at a time. Answering the call to serve my wife, however, is not the checking off of tasks; it's a way of life fueled by a heart of unconditional love. It's a humble posture, otherwise known as submission. When I started writing this book, I thought I knew something about that. I soon discovered I was very, very wrong.

Writer's Block

So many times I sat down to write this chapter and would just freeze in front of the keyboard. I would hear the clock on the wall ticking, take a sip of water, and just sit there with my fingers planted on my keyboard. For all my natural-born creativity, I couldn't figure out exactly how those submission passages from the Bible had worked themselves out in my marriage—at least in a positive way.

At one point I decided to write a story from Raquel's and my marriage that related to submission. I desperately hoped the inspiration would flow from there. But it didn't work. I wrote this rambling chapter about one time that I totally ignored Raquel when we were making a major decision, but she took a forgiving attitude, and everything turned out OK. Then I tacked on a conclusion about the amazing, submissive heart Raquel has toward the Lord. I felt a little uncomfortable with it, but my deadline for turning in the manuscript was drawing nigh, so I figured we just had to hold our noses and roll with it.

I submitted the chapter to my editor because writer's block (or perhaps a spiritual block) was keeping me from writing anything else. I felt a little panicky about it, but my editor assured me that it couldn't be as bad as I thought. (You've truly never met a more encouraging editor.) She reviewed it and gave me a call. Her verdict: I could take my chapter to the next level by deleting 93 percent of it.

I was stressed, because if my encouraging editor didn't like it, then it was definitely garbage. So, I decided to give up on writing a submission chapter and write something about personal finances instead.

The problem was that a chapter about our journey to financial responsibility would have been basically two sentences: "We have no debt, we pay our credit cards and bills every month, and thanks to a course called Financial Peace University, my 401(k) is doing better than ever. Praise the Lord!" That clearly wasn't going to work.

Raquel caught wind of my intention to bail on the topic, and she encouraged me not to give up. She said she felt certain that the Lord was doing something in my heart through my writing of it. So, I went back to the drawing board. This time, however, I opened my Bible and took a harder look at Ephesians 5:21–24, a passage that makes me very uncomfortable because I've never read anything so politically incorrect.

> Submit to one another out of reverence for Christ. Wives, submit yourselves to your own husbands as you do to the Lord. For the husband is the head of the wife as Christ is the head of the church, his body, of which he is the Savior. Now as the church submits to Christ, so also wives should submit to their husbands in everything.

The part that vexed me the most was verse 21: "Submit to one another out of reverence for Christ." The idea of a man and woman submitting to one another created this uncomfortable tension with the other verses about wives submitting to their husbands in everything. I didn't know what to do with it, and I certainly didn't know what it meant for my marriage. But then I stopped and, in something akin to a Prayer of Examen, looked back on my years with Raquel, and God showed me a few things that shed light on the mystery of submission.

The Cycle of Sacrifice

Raquel has, without question, sacrificed the most for our marriage and family. She left behind an MBA program when we got engaged because it would otherwise stall our wedding. She also chose to stay at home with our three kids and accept the loss of the independence and autonomy she could've had (and that she wanted) outside the home. She will tell you that, despite the losses that came with those decisions, they were worth it because God used both of those circumstances to transform her desires and direct her to the work of ministry that she's pursuing today. The sad thing is, I didn't really appreciate the magnitude of her sacrifice until I started writing this book.

When I thought back on the way I had lived as a husband, my "sacrifice" felt small compared to hers. I mean, I've gotten way better at doing chores with a good attitude. I'm also present with my family when I'm home, and I gladly encourage Raquel to take time away from the house so she can get time by herself or even go on a weekend retreat. But those are things that, for the most part, I'm already willing to do. It doesn't really feel like much of a sacrifice for me. Plus, as I've looked back on my marriage, I've realized just how often I've blown off Raquel when she has insisted that I do something I didn't want to do. If I submitted to her wishes at all, she often had to pester me into it. And by the way, let's keep in mind some of the ways she's asked me to give in: *by happily doing chores, praying with her, using more discretion.* And what was my response?

"Stop trying to tell me what to do all the time."

"Your tone is horrible."

"I'm a grown man, not your child."

As I reflected on our story, I realized that the thing that shook up my view of submission was the heartbreak of getting pummeled by life in our ninth year of marriage. As I've shared in the last three chapters, in the span of a year, I went through a nightmare diet therapy for seizures and developed something akin to an eating disorder. My dad died. My sex life crashed. My job was eating up tons of family time, and I was feeling like a failure as a father and husband. Under the weight of all of it, I spiraled into a dark depression. Where did that leave the man of the house? Broken, needy, and desperate.

Gone were my fantasies of being in control. Instead, my demands for respect had turned into anxious pleas for unconditional love.

After another sexual breakdown: "Please don't give up on me."

At my dad's graveside service: "Please put your hand on my back. I can't stop shaking."

In my desperation for something decent to eat: "Can you please make me some keto bread?"

Sitting on the floor of the bathroom, sobbing: "I can't do this, Raquel. I can't do it. I can't do it."

I couldn't receive such sacrificial love and keep being the husband I had always been. Raquel had laid down her life for me like the church does for Christ. She had poured herself out for my benefit, and in extravagantly doing so, she had provoked a desire in me to lay down my life for her. I didn't just want to defer to her when it was convenient. I wanted to follow her lead and give in when it actually cost me something. Essentially, through her own self-sacrifice, she had started a cycle of mutual submission between us.

Standing Next to Me

There's nothing more I want in life than to see Jesus, to hear Him, to touch Him. That's what I've always wanted since I was a kid. Raquel has given me an opportunity to do that. In the most painful season of my life, I saw Him in her compassionate face. I heard Him in her words of encouragement. I even smelled His kindness in the keto-friendly desserts she prepared for me. Her love brought light to the "dark night of the soul," as John of the Cross called it.

One Sunday morning when I was feeling particularly despondent, I stood in the church service, singing along with the worship music, feeling the weight of grief pulling me down. The thought kept running through my mind, "It's so hard to be alive."

As Raquel and I were standing next to each other, she reached behind me and softly touched my back with her hand, and then she wrapped her arm around my waist and drew me closer to her. For the longest time, she stayed in place, gently reassuring me with her touch. At some point, however, it occurred to me that it wasn't Raquel who was standing next to me anymore—it was, without a doubt in my mind, Jesus. It was truly *Him*. Raquel had vanished, and He had tangibly taken her place. He was right there holding me close when I needed Him more than ever.

Tears started rolling down my cheeks and I prayed, "Jesus, thank You so much for being here right now. I need You so badly." He didn't say anything in response, and He didn't have to. His strong embrace communicated the only thing I really needed to hear: "Joshua, I'm not going anywhere."

Finding God in the Messiness

I'm still trying to figure out what it means to live into my responsibility to be like Christ, the most self-sacrificial Husband of all time. I want to be willing to let go of my insistence that I have it this way or that way. I want to be willing to give up that which is dear to me—opportunities, dreams, and autonomy—if that's what it takes to be a blessing to Raquel and our children. I'd like to be the husband that Raquel hasn't yet had: a man who's so humble and assured in the love of God that he can handle it when his wife is having a bad day and isn't her best self.

As a husband, when I've thought about my increasing desire to submit to God, He has shown me something: That desire didn't originate with me. God is the reason I even want to change, "for it is he who works in [me] to will and to act in order to fulfill his good purpose" (Philippians 2:13). He's been taking Raquel's attempts to get me to change (or submit) and exasperating me to the point that I've given up, bit by bit, and started growing into a man I never imagined I could be: a true representative of Jesus in my marriage.

God was at the Tomb of the Unknown Soldier demonstrating what it felt like to be known and accepted. He led me to turn the spotlight on my own weaknesses with the integrity interviews so that I could see how much I needed to grow. He led Raquel to pressure me into a more disciplined prayer life, and although I resisted, she (and He) didn't give up. He was going to get closer to me, whether I thought I needed it or not. And God wasn't just teaching me to love Raquel better. He brought me into relationship with in-laws, people who pushed me to try to figure out, in a way I never had, what love and honor look like. And in the most desolate hours of my life, He was there behind the face of Raquel, assuring me that His love would never fail me. All of it was part of a grand plan to answer the prayer I've prayed so many times: "Lord, please make me more like You."

And that's just in the first ten years.

I wonder what God has been doing in your relationship with your spouse over the past year or month or even yesterday. Do you find yourself agitated? Are you frustrated that the two of you keep going around the same mountain and never getting anywhere? Don't give up on yourselves. God is going round and round that mountain with you. Take a look around, staying alert as the two of you go on this journey of submissive self-sacrifice. And don't be surprised when you discover God's unexpected graces in the midst of all the beautifully messy places of your marriage.

9

The Last Word
(From the Author's Wife)

It's not often that an author extends an invitation to his wife to have the last word in a book he has spent more than a year writing. But we knew it wasn't going to be complete unless I shared some of my own "confessions" about what God has been doing in me during our first decade of marriage.

Let me start by acknowledging how much I appreciate Joshua's generous descriptions of me. They do not come as a surprise. From the time we began dating, he has lavished praise on me. These affirmations are something that I've had to slowly learn to receive over the past twelve years. This is because—although most of them have been gifts—they have also made me uncomfortable at times, especially when he praises me in front of others.

Typically when he affirms me publicly, I care way too much about appearances. I'm afraid people are going to judge him and think he's bragging. Or I'm afraid someone might take offense or feel uncomfortable. For example, if he affirms me in a way that another woman wishes her husband would affirm her but doesn't, I am sensitive to that. Basically, I care way too much about the "what-ifs" instead of receiving Joshua's unashamed affirmation of me.

I guess I can partly hide behind being more introverted than he is, but then again, Joshua is seriously one of the most extroverted people I've ever met. Putting myself out there is still an area where I'm growing, so it's remarkable that I was OK with him writing this book.

Recently, he affirmed me in a way that topped any public display of affection he had previously lavished on me, and I reacted in a way that I regret. We were on a beach vacation with our kids. One morning, which happened to be our anniversary, Joshua said he wanted to spend some time on the beach. Little did I know what he was doing out there. He was taking one of the kids' plastic shovels and carving in massive letters the message "I LOVE U, RAQUEL!"

When Joshua finished, he ran back to the condominium, took the elevator up to the eighteenth floor, and burst into the room.

"Go look off the balcony!" he said excitedly.

"I'm making a sandwich."

"Honey, please go look out there."

He was like a kid at Christmas. Finally, I walked over to the balcony and saw the message carved into the sand, large enough for everyone in the twenty-story condominium to read.

"That's embarrassing," I said coldly.

"Come on, honey," Joshua said, "I did it for you. I was hoping you'd like it. It's our anniversary."

I felt embarrassed by how public his message was, and Joshua could see it in my face. I could also see the look of disappointment on his, and I understood why: I had pushed him away like so many times before when he tried to lavish love upon me. I resisted instead of giving in to his childlike affection.

"Joshua," I said.

He looked over at me and I could see the frustration in his eyes.

"I'm sorry. The way I responded was so unloving. I don't know what else to say. I have issues."

"I forgive you, Raquel," he said. "But I want you to look out at that beach. Do you see that message? Jesus is the One who wrote that for you. He just used my hands and a plastic shovel to say it as extravagantly as possible. I think it's hard for you to receive love from me because it's hard for you to receive love from Him."

At that moment, it hit me. I felt an awareness of God's presence with us on the balcony. As I stared at the giant "I LOVE U, RAQUEL!" the message felt so lavish, even coming from God. I knew He was confronting me with the truth—the truth of how easily I can reject His love. The truth that His love for me is extravagant—as immeasurable as the grains of sand in which the message was carved, as vast and deep as the ocean behind it. I stood there for a while savoring the moment, humbled yet in awe of how directly God had just spoken to me through Joshua.

At the Beach with Jesus

In the Gospels, Jesus had a moment of truth with Peter on the beach. Beforehand, Jesus had warned Peter that he would deny Him three times. When Jesus was arrested, Peter was questioned by three different people who asked whether he knew Jesus. Peter denied knowing Him. After the third time he did so, a rooster crowed. Scripture reveals a sad scene: "The Lord turned and looked straight at Peter. Then Peter remembered the word the Lord had spoken to him: 'Before the rooster crows today, you will disown me three times.' And he went outside and wept bitterly" (Luke 22:61–62).

The Lord turned and looked straight at Peter . . .

I wonder what Jesus' look was like toward Peter. I imagine it was similar to His expression a few days later when, after His resurrection, He met with Peter on the beach and initiated an intimate exchange. Three times Jesus asked Peter, "Do you love Me?" After the third time, Peter responded: "Lord, you know everything; you know that I love you" (John 21:17 ESV). Jesus turned this loving confrontation into a moment of restoration.

In my own beach story, Jesus was inviting me, like Peter, to a moment of truth and redemption. The God who knows everything about me—even the things I try to hide—was turning and looking directly at me, telling me, "I love you, Raquel!" in the letters Joshua had carved into the sand. He was exposing the truth of my impulsive rejection of His love—and of Joshua's love.

We don't always get such direct messages from God in the midst of everyday life. But He's always present and sharing His love for us in innumerable ways. The question is, Are we taking the time to look for how He shows up in the ordinary?

Looking Back with Eyes of Wonder

This book is the result of Joshua sitting on his own beach with Jesus. It is a prayerful review of our marriage from Joshua's perspective. It is a grand examination of the first ten years of our marriage (Joshua talks about the Prayer of Examen in chapter 4). In the writing process, Joshua rewound the film of our years together to the very beginning. And as he looked at our relationship through the years, he reflected on moments of God's presence in his journey of self-awareness and transformation. This is also something I practice in my own personal walk with God.

God initiates relationship with us throughout the day, and His movements toward me often go over my head. But on many evenings, I like to practice the Prayer of Examen to reflect on my day with God, to pay attention to how He was at work so I don't miss it. This is a response to His presence in my life. I consider both the gifts and the areas of dissonance and recognize areas where I walked with Him and where I resisted Him. I look at the places where I felt alive and the places where I felt drained.

I love the way a wise friend describes this practice: "It's not a modern technique but an old practice of prayer. As you practice examining your own life with God, the goal is to see how the choices we make, the attitudes we adopt, and the things that happen to us move us toward or away from God."

As we practice reflecting back with God, over time, our awareness of Him increases, and we begin to see His presence more in our daily lives. We can also do this in our marriages; it's a way of abiding in Him together. He is the third strand, the third person; He is the One who holds us together (Ecclesiastes 4:12; Colossians 1:17). Much like Peter meeting with Jesus on the beach, we can look to the One who knows our marriages intimately, sit with Him, and allow Him to change us.

As I sit with God in my own marriage, I am filled with gratitude. Although you've read about many places of tension between me and Joshua, I am confident that God has been clearly at work in putting us together and has manifested the mystery of Christ in us. I not only love Joshua, but I like him. And although he's driven me crazy at times, I've never felt a moment when I wanted him to go away. I really enjoy his presence; he is a true companion in every way, and I can honestly say my journey in marriage has been a lot of fun.

But God has also used our weaknesses to bring transformation in my life. I used to be someone who, on the surface, was "too cool for school," but it was only because I was trying so hard to control my image before others. Since I surrendered my life to God, He has been gently leading me toward freedom to be myself. For that reason, being married to someone who rattles my need for control has been a gift. Joshua's audacious personality has brought moments that, at the time, made me feel uneasy, but when I look back, they were times I needed to loosen up.

There is never a dull moment in our home. Joshua's freedom to express love and his passionate pursuit of life have given me the freedom to be myself and to be fully known, fully accepted, and fully loved by him and by God.

I still have a tendency to put Joshua down when I'm walking in insecurity, control, or fear. But as I've grown in humility and the love of Christ, caring less and less about others' opinions of us, I've become more loving, gentle, and kind, even in the midst of tense moments in my marriage. When I stumble, I am much quicker to admit my wrong.

Avoiding Exposure

Growing up, I didn't hear very much about confession. Confession was something people were supposed to do before they asked Jesus into their hearts. At most, I saw it as something that was just between God and me, and even this rarely happened. I somehow overlooked the full process of confession in Scripture: "Confess your sins to each other and pray for each other so that you may be healed" (James 5:16). It's a two-part deal, and early in our marriage, it was something I had to learn from Joshua.

In the early years of marriage, I was easily tempted not to take responsibility for my own actions. I clung to my need to be right, so Joshua was always the first to confess and apologize. He had a lot of room to grow, but as he kept setting the example of acknowledging his wrong, he won me over, and I eventually started following his lead. As I've grown in self-awareness, I've tried to make it a regular practice to look back and reflect on my day or week; while thanking God for the different ways He has been good to me, I also confess my brokenness and the ways I resist God, Joshua, and others.

In *The Mystery of Marriage*, Mike Mason writes about how marriage reveals who we really are:

> One of the hardest things in marriage is the feeling of being watched. It is the constant surveillance that can get to one, that can wear one down like a bright light shining in the eyes, and that leads inevitably to the crumbling of all defenses, all facades, all the customary shams and masquerades of the personality. . . . It makes scant difference whether the watcher be love or something more sinister. What is hard is the watchfulness.

"Like a bright light shining in the eyes" is what marriage can feel like as God uses it to illuminate my sins, defenses, and pretenses. Whether my issues are related to my husband or not, I cannot hide them from him. I can try. But I've discovered that hiding anything becomes exhausting over time and drives a wedge into our relationship. Outside of my home, I can pretend that I'm all put together. But Joshua knows the real me. And I can either blame him for my struggles or I can admit my false ways of living, embrace Christ's forgiveness, and receive the extravagant love God desires to give. Every day I have the choice to find God in the ordinary and extraordinary moments of my life and ask the Holy Spirit what He wants me to notice. And in this process of meeting with God in prayerful reflection, I am transformed.

Back to the Baby Monitor

Let's go back to the baby monitor story Joshua shared in the introduction ("The Story We Absolutely Had to Tell"). My grandmother and aunt heard us through a baby monitor having a heated and immature argument. We had neglected to turn off the speaker in the other room and ended up embarrassing ourselves.

We thought we could conceal our sin behind a closed door; instead, we exposed it utterly. I sure didn't apologize, though. I didn't confess to any wrongdoing on my part. In my mind, Joshua had started everything. I was pointing the finger at him. In that moment, I was like Adam and Eve when they got caught in their sin. "They heard the sound of the LORD God walking in the garden at the time of the evening breeze, and the man and his wife hid themselves from the presence of the LORD God among the trees of the garden" (Genesis 3:8 NRSV).

When God asked them about it, Eve blamed Satan and never confessed or apologized to Adam, let alone God. Like Eve, I threw on fig leaves by *pretending* that nothing had happened in a desperate attempt to act like everything was OK.

I have found that my pretending is the opposite of the freedom I have in Christ. Our gracious God lovingly exposes our sin in a multitude of ways. We have the choice to ignore and reject those loving messages or embrace them and receive forgiveness.

As I invite Jesus into those moments, I find treasures in the dark places. Isaiah 45:3 says, "And I will give you treasures hidden in the darkness—secret riches. I will do this so you may know that I am the LORD, the God of Israel, the one who calls you by name" (NLT).

In my beach story, I felt ashamed to admit my impulsive denial of both Joshua's and God's love toward me. But as I invited Jesus into this dark place in my heart, I found the treasure of uninhibited love from God, who knows everything about me and who gave me a loving, unashamed, and affirming husband.

Sharing Your Brokenness

As Joshua was writing this book, a few people seemed alarmed. "You're letting him tell all of this?" they asked. My answer: Absolutely! I feel that an authentic book like this is a gift. We often don't see real marriages on social media, which portrays a highly varnished version of matrimony. In this book, Joshua has shown that while our marriage is not perfect, and we are not perfect, God has held us together in the midst of all we do and loves us continually.

Joshua and our marriage have been exposed in this book. You might ask, "What about discretion and privacy? Why share your personal business?" My answer: None of us can hide.

If you're honest, you can see the things Joshua talks about in people around you, and the truth is that others can see it in you too. The Bible is filled with raw stories of people, chosen by God, who were flawed and sinful. And yet God lovingly exposed their sin and glorified Himself through them. This is the gospel and the work of the Kingdom of God in our lives.

Finding God in the Messiness

It's easy to read about someone else's vulnerability and choose not to be vulnerable yourself. My prayer for you, the reader, is the same prayer I have for myself: that we will more willingly spend time with God in authenticity and in gratitude, confessing our sins to Him and to other believers, so that we may be healed (James 5:16). May we not lose the opportunity to allow God to redeem what was broken in the garden. May we be bold to approach God and not only let go of the fig leaves of pretense that we put on but also look into the eyes of the One who *knows us* and sees us through the lens of love.

Thanks be to Jesus Christ, who has covered the sin in our marriage, taken our shame, and forgiven all of the brokenness that you have seen in our story. He also does the same in your story. As we invite Jesus in, we do what is described in Psalm 139:23–24. I love this translation:

Investigate my life, O God, find out everything about me; cross-examine and test me, get a clear picture of what I'm about; see for yourself whether I've done anything wrong—then guide me on the road to eternal life. (MSG)

As you close this book, may you meet with Jesus at the beach in the evening breezes of your life. I invite you to reflect back on your day and even your own marriage in a Prayer of Examen. Pause and close your eyes, and with an awareness of God's love for you, rewind your day with Him. Wait on Him as you ask yourself the following questions, which Joshua suggested in chapter 4:

- What was I most grateful for today?
- What was I least grateful for?
- Did I feel myself walking in step with the Lord at any point?
- Did I resist God at any point?
- Was there anything that was particularly life-giving?
- Was there anything that drained me?
- Where did I give and receive the most love?
- Where did I give and receive the least love?

You don't have to ask yourself every one of these questions. If you'd prefer, you can just ask yourself, "When was I was aware of God in my day? In what way am I aware of God in my marriage?"

As you ponder these questions with God, invite Him to help you answer them honestly. Pay attention as you prayerfully think through your day. See if the Holy Spirit brings to mind some aspect of your life, your character, or your marriage, and ask Him to reveal what He may want to show you in that area. As you reveal yourself for who you really are, you'll see Him more and more for who He really is: the One who loves you completely. And in that holy space, may you catch glimpses of being in Eden.

—*Raquel L. Rogers*

Epilogue

When I signed up to write this book, I never anticipated what a gift it would be to review the first decade of my marriage and share some of the insights I've gleaned along the way. As it turns out, I actually learned quite a lot during the process of writing the book itself. There were *Aha!* moments as I wrote and rewrote, edited, deleted entire chapters (three times in one case), and replaced them with more meaningful thoughts. One of the biggest moments of revelation happened when I did an *examen* after the chapters had been completed.

As I came before God for this time of self-examination, I first asked myself, *What am I most grateful for from my first decade of marriage?* That was easy. I remembered time after time when Raquel had sacrificially loved me. The first example that came to my mind was the moment when I was sitting on the bathroom floor with my face buried in my hands, brushing away tears as Raquel sat next to me in silence. I had lowered my guard and revealed my dark, depressive state; and she had drawn close to me with tenderness and sensitivity. She simply loved me when I was at my lowest instead of being exasperated at my inability to pull myself together.

I also felt gratitude when I asked myself, *How did I move in step with the Lord over the past ten years of marriage?* I had given in and drawn closer to God in my spiritual life, laying down my pride and actually accepting the fact that Raquel had a lot to teach me about growing spiritually. Yet, it stung when I pondered the question, *How did I resist God during the past decade of marriage?* I knew that I had exhausted Raquel with my stubbornness and my persistent attempts to maintain control of my life. I had often disregarded her needs and considered mine more important than hers. And the worst part was that it wasn't just an occasional problem—it was a consistent pattern.

As I reviewed memory after memory, I was heartbroken to see just how heavily the balance of surrender to God versus resistance to Him was skewed in favor of refusing to submit to Him. It was a humiliating blow to acknowledge that, for all of the ways I've grown, there are plenty of times that I still cling tightly to my crown, resisting the call to relinquish the throne of my heart to the King of kings, the Husband of all husbands. And in the face of that sobering revelation, I felt the Lord put His finger on my heart, and I knew what He was saying in the silence: *Do you love Me? Show that by being more loving to Raquel.*

As I absorbed the gravity of my need to grow, I began to imagine what it would look like to change as a husband. What if I gave up control when it came to making decisions, big and small? What if I listened more and talked less? Perhaps I could do a better job of overlooking offenses instead of constantly reminding Raquel of the areas in which she needs to grow.

While I liked the idea of changing, it was too overwhelming, too unrealistic to seriously consider. I'm too set in my ways. I change too slowly. I just can't be the husband I want to be—the husband Raquel deserves. And in response to my despair, the Lord reminded me that "My grace is sufficient for you, for My strength is made perfect in weakness" (2 Corinthians 12:9 NKJV). That verse came alive to me in a new way as I realized that my weakness as a husband is actually an asset. When I invite the Lord to face those weaknesses with me, I move closer to a place of total dependence on Him. And at the same time, I keep growing into the spouse He wants me to be.

I find so much hope in Hebrews 10:14: "For by one sacrifice [God] has made perfect forever those who are being made holy." That means that being a good husband isn't about arriving; it's about drawing near to the One who shed His blood so that I could be in a continual process of "being made holy." And when all is said and done, I want *that* to be the story of my years as a husband—the story of a man who became more loving to his wife as he became a more loving son to his heavenly Father. I want to replay my marriage over and over in the decades to come and, with great joy, proclaim, "Look what the Lord has done."

—*Joshua L. Rogers*

APPENDIX A

Look at Your Own Marriage

LEARNING THINGS ABOUT MARRIAGE FROM ANOTHER PERSON'S story is one thing, but taking a closer look at your *own* story is a whole other matter. Go back through some of the big ideas from each chapter, reflect on them by answering a few questions, and use the suggested prayer prompts as you ask God how to become more aware of His work in your marriage.

Chapter 1: In the Beginning

Your story began long before you and your spouse ever met. The beautiful and not-so-beautiful aspects of your backstories can reveal a road map of God's sovereignty in bringing the two of you together. Think about the story of your life before you and your spouse got to know each other. . . .

1. What lessons (positive or negative) did I learn early on from my parents' relationship?
2. What are some things that brought me shame before I met my spouse? Were they sins committed against me? Were they sins that I committed against others?
3. Have I ever told my spouse the less attractive parts of my pre-relationship story? If so, how did my spouse respond? If not, how do I think it could benefit the relationship to do so?

Father, You know the details of my story, and You have used each twist and turn to bring me to my spouse. Thank You for that. If there's any long-standing shame that I've been keeping from my spouse, help me understand why I hide it. Help me see how You've used all things—even the unlovely things—to work together for my good and for the good of my marriage.

Chapter 2: Reality Sets In

At some point in your relationship with your spouse, weaknesses and character flaws eventually emerge. In the everyday power struggles, big and small, you have to decide whether you're willing to let go of control and overlook some of the offenses that naturally come with closeness. Your willingness to love (or failure to do so) can reveal how serious you are about unconditional love. Think back to when you began discovering your spouse's most agitating weaknesses and character flaws. . . .

1. Do I pray for my spouse in the areas where I see growth is needed?
2. Do I encourage my spouse as much as I criticize him or her? Do I encourage my spouse at all? If not, what might be holding me back?
3. What are three things I appreciate about my spouse? Am I willing to share them in meaningful ways?

Father, I'm well aware of my spouse's weaknesses. If I've let those weaknesses define the way I view my spouse, I confess that to You. Please give me the grace to see the many good qualities that are there too. Show me areas in my own life where I need to grow. Teach me to speak words of life over my spouse, even when I need to address a weakness.

Chapter 3: Stunned by My Reflection

Seeing your spouse's blind spots is easy, but what about yours? As uncomfortable as it may be, one of the most valuable things you can do for your marriage is ask your spouse what kind of impact you have on the emotional climate of your home. If you're simply willing to ask, you might be surprised by the things—both positive and negative—you discover. . . .

1. What might happen if I ask my spouse for feedback about what it's like to live with me? How does it feel to consider asking my spouse such a question?
2. What are some of the things I'm afraid my spouse will say if I open myself to receiving feedback?
3. Am I willing to sit down and ask my spouse (without defending myself), "Where do I have room to grow?" and "What are some of the ways I'm a blessing to you?"

God, You know all of my blind spots, and my spouse knows many of them as well. When You use my spouse to open my eyes to the ways I need to change, help me to be receptive. Give me the grace to overlook poor delivery or negative emotion that may be lurking behind my spouse's feedback. I want to grow, God. Give me the humility to learn from my spouse so that I can change.

Chapter 4: Prayer Pressure

Spiritual intimacy is, in many ways, like emotional or sexual intimacy. You and your spouse can skip out on it, but it will have a negative effect on your marriage. Sometimes trying to engage with your spouse spiritually can feel unnatural and awkward—like something reserved for super spiritual couples. But with a little practice, spiritual intimacy can become a thriving part of your marriage. The most important thing is to keep trying and learning as you go. Think about the various ways you and your spouse engage with each other spiritually (even if it's just going to church occasionally). . . .

1. What are my expectations for what my spiritual life with my spouse should look like? How realistic are they considering where we are now?

2. How do I feel when my spouse and I try to engage spiritually? If I'm not engaging with my spouse spiritually, what's the reason for that?

3. What is one thing my spouse and I can do to draw closer to God together? Am I willing to do this one thing?

Father, I want to be closer to You and closer to my spouse. Give us the grace to want to be more spiritually connected. Show us ways we can grow closer to You as a couple. Help us to do just one thing to grow in our spiritual life together.

Chapter 5: Grace and the In-Laws

Working through personality differences in your marriage can be daunting enough, but the in-laws can bring their own set of challenges and joys into the life you're building as a couple. Either way, it comes as part of the marriage package, which may come as a pleasant or unpleasant surprise. Think about your in-laws (even the ones who are no longer alive), including your spouse's extended family. . . .

1. Regardless of how I feel about my in-laws, do I speak positively about them in front of my spouse and others? How could doing so positively affect my marriage?

2. What are some ways I can connect to my in-laws, regardless of whether we have chemistry?

3. Have I tried praying for my in-laws? How could that positively impact my relationship with my spouse?

If you have an excellent relationship with your in-laws, take this opportunity to thank God for that. If not, consider this prayer:

Father, You sent Jesus to earth to fit in with a world full of people who were very different from Him. If He loved us while we were still sinners, I trust He can help me love my in-laws. Show my spouse and me how to love our families well and in the healthiest way possible.

Chapter 6: Naked and Ashamed

Physical intimacy is as essential to a happy marriage as meaningful conversations, quality time, and spiritual connection. Sometimes sex is fantastically pleasurable; other times it may feel like you're going through the motions. Either way, if your focus is on loving your spouse, sex is a bold declaration that nothing is going to tear you two apart. Take a minute to think about your current sex life and how you are (or are not) making it a loving experience. . . .

1. Am I motivated or apathetic about making love to my spouse? What kind of message does that send to my spouse?

2. How can I be considerate of my spouse's sexual needs in a way I have not practiced in the past?

3. Is there anyone or anything other than my spouse
   that is meeting my emotional or physical needs in an
   intimate way?

Father, thank You for the amazing, beautiful gift of sex! Thank You for how it mysteriously bonds my spouse and me together as a couple. When I have sex with my spouse, I want to do it with a heart of unconditional love. If I find myself feeling apathetic about sex, give me the grace to see it as the gift that You made it to be. Help me think of my spouse's needs and not just my own. Give us the will and the strength to resist all of the forces that seek to keep us from experiencing the unity You intend for us.

Chapter 7: For Better or Worse

It's likely that either you or your spouse tend to be the strong one and the other the more emotionally dependent one. We all encounter struggles, which should drive us to Jesus and our spouse for support. Problems arise, though, when you and/or your spouse are not honest about your struggles. When you come together in the hard times and invite Jesus into the mess, He can become the third strand in your relationship and make both of you stronger. Think about the ways you and your spouse are willing to be emotionally vulnerable with each other. . . .

1. Am I generally the strong one or the weak one in our
   relationship? What would it look like for me to break out
   of that role and occasionally step into a different one?

2. Do I have a Christian peer or a counselor who is helping shoulder any burdens I carry, or is my spouse the only one I lean on to meet all of my emotional needs? How might it help to allow others in my community to offer emotional support?

3. How can I be more vulnerable with my spouse today?

Father, I want my marriage to have a healthy balance of emotional need-meeting. Help my spouse and me to be honest about the ways we're struggling and to find support outside our marriage when we need it. We need You, each other, and other people. Please help us humbly accept help when we need it.

Chapter 8: Fully Submitted

There's more to biblical submission than figuring out who gets to call the shots when it comes to decision-making. Marriage is a living analogy in which the husband plays the part of Jesus and the wife plays the part of the church. That's no small task for either spouse. Both are called to sacrifice for the sake of their beloved (though Jesus carries the infinitely greater burden). As you and your spouse willingly and sacrificially surrender to one another, it creates a cycle of mutual submission that honors both God and your marriage. Think about the relational dynamic between you and your spouse. . . .

1. Is our relationship characterized by a regular, mutual effort to love without strings attached?

2. Who tends to call the shots in our marriage? What factors play into this?

3. When have I put my spouse's needs before my own and taken pleasure in it? What is one way (even if it's small) that I can begin to put my spouse's needs before my own?

Father, I want to be in control of my life sometimes, and I do so at the expense of my spouse. Frankly, Lord, I often think that my needs are more important than my spouse's needs. Show me how to love my spouse radically and unreservedly. I want to take pleasure in laying down my life, but I can only do that through the power of Your Holy Spirit. Fill me, Lord. Show me how to live out my role in the divine romance of Jesus and His bride.

Chapter 9: The Last Word

One of the ways Jesus shows His love for us is through compassionate confrontation. But we only get to have those kinds of encounters with Him when we welcome Him to see us for who we really are. Coming before Him in prayerful self-examination (*examen*) is an opportunity to come face-to-face with what our daily life is actually like—not what we wish it was like. In that place, we can issue a unique invitation for God to do His redemptive work in our marriages and our individual lives. Imagine what it would be like for you to bring your whole self to God by inviting Him into every aspect of your life, including your role as spouse. . . .

1. Do I open myself to God and reveal everything about myself? Do I even know myself?
2. Am I willing to see things in my life and my marriage for what they really are? If that feels intimidating, why?
3. When I replay yesterday in my mind like a movie, do I notice a time when God was present in my marriage? Did I resist walking with Him at any point?

Search me, Lord, and know my heart. I don't even know my heart, Father. I often float through the day, just trying to make it until bed-time. What's going on with me? What's going on with my marriage? Please give me the grace and the energy to spend a few minutes reviewing my daily life with You. Remind me that when all is said and done, nothing will be more important to me than knowing You.

APPENDIX B

How to Do the Integrity Interview

I've encountered countless men and women to do the "Integrity Interview" I talk about in chapter 3. The only person who has tried it is Raquel. Most people say something like the following: "That sounds awful—I would never do it. I'm well aware of my flaws. I don't need anyone to tell me what they are."

While that sounds valid, the truth is all of us have blind spots. And being *self-conscious* about your flaws isn't the same as being *self-aware*. Self-conscious people know that there are negative ways they impact others, but they just feel insecure about their flaws and don't change. Self-aware people care enough to learn how they impact the world around them and do something about it.

Keep in mind that while this exercise can result in self-improvement, that's not the purpose. This is primarily an act of caring for the people in our lives. It's a genuine response to the call from Philippians 2:3–4: "In humility value others above yourselves, not looking to your own interests but each of you to the interests of the others."

This is about valuing the people around you enough to learn what changes you can make to be a greater blessing to others (especially your spouse). For that reason, I'd encourage you to prayerfully consider doing these interviews. Before you get started, consider these guidelines that will help you get the most out of the exercise. This is the list my friend Aaron suggested to me:

- Choose to interview people whom you trust—only those who want to see you thrive as a person. Choose people who champion you.
- Ask God to give you the courage and humility to metabolize what you hear and turn the feedback into growth.
- Try to meet in person or by video chat (not by phone, and definitely not by email exchange).
- Try to interview at least four people (if you interview someone and they only have positive things to say, you need to interview someone else).

- Use a journal, legal pad, or laptop to record what you learn during your interviews.
- Only ask follow-up questions in order to learn more or clarify what the interviewee is trying to tell you. Don't try to defend yourself, explain yourself, or offer your perspective.
- Review your notes, summarize them, and schedule a time to talk with a close friend, pastor, or mentor about your findings.

The questions I asked were a modification of the ones suggested by Dr. Henry Cloud in the book *Integrity*, and some are from Aaron. These questions include the following:

1. What is it like being around me when I'm at my best?
2. What is it like being around me when I'm at my worst?
3. What do you admire about the way I live my life?
4. Are there any areas of my life that you find off-putting?
5. What are ways I could be a better friend and/or spouse?
6. Which of my character traits is a blessing?
7. Which of my character traits is a burden?
8. Is there anything I could do to be a better communicator?
9. What are some positive and negative ways I impact others?
10. What is the "10 percent" you're holding back?

I realize that this list may look intimidating, maybe even terrifying, but keep in mind that the questions also give you an opportunity to learn about the ways you're a blessing to others. You might be surprised to learn what those ways are.

I encourage you to accompany this exercise with the Prayer of Examen that I described in chapter 4. With this prayer, you invite God to meet you in the reality of what your life is really like, asking yourself questions like "Where did I walk in step with God today?" or "Where did I find myself resisting God?" Usually, a Prayer of Examen is something that you do as you review the previous day, but it's also something you can do in a broader review of your life, as I've done with my marriage in this book. The point is that it's not enough to invite other people to give you unvarnished insight about yourself. You also need to peel back the layers for God, let Him reveal the areas where He's at work, and rest in His unconditional love for you. As the old Sunday school song goes, "How loving and patient He must be, 'cause He's still working on me." He's never going to give up on you. Don't give up on yourself.

Fear is the only obstacle keeping you or anyone else from doing an exercise like this. Like Adam and Eve, our desire to conceal our brokenness only keeps us from handing it over to God and letting Him do something good with it. Being free from shame gives us the power to declare that, yes, we need to change, but praise God that He "makes us more and more like him as we are changed into his glorious image" (2 Corinthians 3:18 NLT).

Let me extend a word of caution: If there's one mistake I made when I did the interviews, it's that I didn't seek enough help processing the feedback, and I really needed it. Looking in the mirror and seeing so many ugly things I had been hiding from myself was devastating. Sure, I had a couple of good friends with whom I verbally processed, but that wasn't enough. If you're going to address long-term problems, you really need someone with the wisdom to help you sort it out, whether a pastor, counselor, spiritual director, or mentor. But even though I didn't do that, I still wouldn't trade the positive effects of those interviews with my friends for anything.

Like Proverbs 20:30 says, "Blows that hurt cleanse away evil, as do stripes the inner depths of the heart" (NKJV). Essentially, it comes down to whether I'm willing to love and be loved in a way that hurts me enough to push me to help others. As I've chosen to appreciate the cleansing pain of hard feedback and be grateful for the people who've brought it through my integrity interviews, I've embraced some cleansing in the inner depths of my heart. And in my marriage, it has helped me change in ways that all the conflict in the world couldn't accomplish.

Acknowledgments

When I was in the sixth grade, my mother bought me a typewriter—a real one from Sears. It was called "The Communicator." It sits on the credenza in my office, where people frequently enter and look at it with fascination.

"Wow, look at that," they say and then touch the keys.

I'll never let go of that typewriter. It reminds me of the fact that I haven't gotten where I am today without the help of countless people—and not just the people whom I'll thank below. I'm talking about those people who, from my childhood, have called out the gifts that the Lord put in me, and they've done it by walking in their own callings. For each of you, I am grateful, and I am particularly grateful for the following friends and family:

I'll begin with Raquel Rogers, my dear companion, the one who has shown me the love of Jesus more deeply than anyone else I've known. Raquel, I hope that people read the pages of this book and see Jesus in you like I have. Thank you for allowing me to tell our story—*God's* story in our lives. Thank you a thousand times over for all the hours you sacrificed so that I could work on this gargantuan project. You are a gift—far more than I thought God would ever give me. Thank you for choosing me.

To my parents, Paula and David: Thank you for your marriage, for all the songs we sang together, the time we spent on our knees as a family. Thank you for teaching me the Bible. Thank you for showing me what it means to try as hard as you can when your marriage faces insurmountable obstacles, and when you can't try anymore, to love the best you can anyway. It is one of the great privileges of my life to have been your son, to love and be loved by you so unreservedly.

To Shon and Beth Cunningham: This book could never do justice to the gift you have been to me. Shon, think of the countless thousands of hours you've listened to me. You often said little, but that's because you were being so careful to speak what the Holy Spirit put on your heart. Most importantly, thank you both for helping me believe in love again.

To Suzanne Gosselin, our dear friend and editor: There are no words to convey our gratitude to you. This is not just the Rogerses' book; it is yours. No one who reads this book will ever be able to appreciate the way your discernment in editing this book helped form its character. Thank you for drawing melodies out of my writing that I could've never sung on my own.

To Aaron Damiani: I still marvel that God allowed me to have such a windfall with a friend like you. People only dream of having a friend who is such an earnest listener, a strong, kind man of childlike enthusiasm in your love for the Lord and others. Thank you for giving me the gift of your vulnerability and for treating with such care the vulnerability I have given you.

To Martha Renaud and Lisa Anderson from Boundless.org and Lynne Jordal-Martin from Fox News: The three of you have been more than editors over the years; you have been friends to me. You gave me a chance, cheered me on, and took me under your wings, where I've grown as a writer. To use a favorite phrase of yours, Lynne, you were three of God's "messengers." Without the three of you helping me become a better "messenger" of my own, this book would not have happened.

To Robert Wolgemuth: You've been so much more than an agent. You've been a friend in the faith who shepherded me through the process of finding a great company like Worthy Publishing. You caught the vision for this book, told me to run with it, and never stopped cheering for me like I was your own son. Thank you so much.

To my children, Giselle, Layla, and Isaiah: I had so much trouble working on this book when you were in the house, and do you know why? Because I couldn't help myself—I wanted to be with you. I *love* being with you. Did you notice that there were many times I let the three of you climb all over me like monkeys while I was writing? It's because you three little monkeys are part of what kept me joyfully going during this journey to tell part of the story of your mom and me. Thank you for that.

Finally, to all the people who've prayed for me or encouraged me over the years as I've grown as a writer (including so many on social media), thank you. There have been days when I've wondered if my writing really matters, and God used your prayers or encouragement to lift my spirit and keep me going. I pray God will surround you with people who care for you in the unseen ways you've cared for me.

I'm going to keep on writing, and as I do, I'll remain thankful for all of you. You really can't do anything that matters if you don't have loving people walking alongside you.

About the Author

JOSHUA ROGERS is a husband, a father of three, an attorney, and a writer. He has been published at FoxNews.com, the *Washington Post*, *Christianity Today* (CT.com), and Boundless.org (a ministry of Focus on the Family). He has also garnered two Evangelical Press Association awards. Over the past fourteen years, he has served as both a civil and criminal prosecutor. You can read more of his writing at JoshuaRogers.com and follow him @MrJoshuaRogers on both Facebook and Twitter.